'This is not a dramatic tale of overcoming incredible adversity or surviving some kind of disaster. No loves have been lost, no hearts broken. This is a rather ordinary tale, of finding myself and forming a ritual of self-care that I like to call Saturday Night Pasta.'

———

Saturday Night Pasta is therapy for the modern-day food lover, teaching self-care through the humble act of making pasta. Like the practice of meditation, making pasta by hand is a way of achieving self-discovery and mindfulness ... with delicious results. Including stories, mantras, step-by-step guides to different pasta shapes, trouble-shooting tips and 40 irresistible, comforting recipes (with dried pasta substitutes for the time poor), this is a cookbook to inspire and empower.

SNP

Saturday Night Pasta

Elizabeth Hewson

Photography by Nikki To

plum ·  Pan Macmillan Australia

My favourite form of comfort,
apart from making pasta, is my little family.
To Tom, Forest and now Louis,
thank you for being my security blanket.

Contents

Introduction

Do you ever feel anxious? I do.

It's so easy to fall into the trap of anxiety – that all too familiar, all-consuming and often paralysing state of being.

Like many people, I have struggled with work–life balance throughout my career. It is a complex matter, especially for those of us who live to work, rather than work to live. Emotional attachment can make work a major part of your identity. That's not necessarily a bad thing, but the danger is allowing it to take over your identity completely.

Whether we like to admit it or not, self-doubt and the need for approval from others can take over if we are not careful. For a long time, my sense of self was based on my performance, my productivity and how others perceived me. Anxiety was the result – and it still comes in moments. Writing this book has found me once again asking myself, 'Am I good enough?'

I thought I had these feelings in check until a couple of years ago, when again I felt that I was losing control. All of a sudden, a stressful work situation exacerbated my anxiety, leaving me crippled by a constant state of worry. I would panic and overthink situations to the point where I lost my confidence. I would wake up throughout the night with my mind racing. Even getting out of bed in the morning became a challenge, my head filled with trepidation at the thought of the day that lay before me. I found myself turning to all the recommended methods of coping – exercise, yoga, I even bought a puppy to try to calm my nerves. But in the end, what it took was the simple act of making pasta.

————

I have always counted myself lucky to have discovered my interests early in life, establishing a love for food and restaurants while at university. This appetite pushed me to seek out a job where I got to work with some of the most creative minds in Australian hospitality. I thrived and it drove me to be productive and ambitious, always hungry to learn more about food. But I was also restless, I wanted to experience more and so decided to broaden my horizons.

I have always felt a strong connection to Italy – its soul, warmth, traditions – and it was a culture I wanted to immerse myself in; a spirit I wanted to absorb. Never one to do things by halves, I signed up to do a year-long Masters degree in food culture and communication at the University of Gastronomic Sciences in Piedmont, the birthplace of the Slow Food movement. I packed my bags and headed to a small town in Italy's northwest, leaving behind a great job, my fiancé Tom and a comfortable existence. For some reason, a leap into the largely unknown felt just right.

The course was comprehensive, exploring food through multiple lenses, such as law, sustainable agriculture, philosophy, tourism, anthropology, chemistry, history and writing. We studied artisanal foods in intense detail, spending days at a time learning about cheese, wine, beer, cured meats and chocolate. We shared ideas, recipes, food – cooking meals for each other from our own cultures. We went to aperitivo every night. We embraced seasonality and simplicity in food. And then there was the pasta. I discovered the magic of pasta from scenes of nonne hand-making piles of agnolotti, the range of fresh pastas available at every supermarket and the endless bowls I devoured at the local osterie. There was a pasta for every occasion, every moment, every feeling.

It was the first time I had ever really been alone. I had never travelled or lived by myself, so feelings of loneliness came and went over the course of that year. This taught me more about myself and how to appreciate my own company with a sense of confidence that would stand me in good stead down the track.

Upon my return, I secured my dream job working in communications for the country's best restaurants. The role was challenging, exciting and inspiring. The people, the food, the industry – I loved it all. I threw myself in and work quickly became very personal, making it hard to separate my life from my career – but strangely it made my anxiety manageable, as I knew I had found my calling.

A few years later, I found myself in an ongoing situation at work that really started to get under my skin and I struggled to manage. The coping strategies I had used up to that point just weren't cutting it this time. I was destabilised, devoid of all my confidence and drive. I would take everything personally, often an innocuous moment would send me into a spiral. So began sleepless nights. Constant negativity. Discomfort. Try as I might to talk myself out of it, anxiety is a peculiar thing. While you may try to reassure yourself over and over, there you are at 11 pm in a full body shudder. I tried to keep this anxiety hidden in the background, but inside it felt like an ever-present bee that buzzed around and around in my head.

I decided I needed to find something outside of work to take my mind off matters. Surely yoga was the answer. I made it to a yoga class, once. There I was, lying down in the back corner, trying to stay as small and unnoticeable as possible. Surrounded by crop tops and flashy lycra outfits, my tights were splattered with dried paint from re-doing the kitchen earlier that month and my baggy, once-white T-shirt was stained from cooking experiments. I told myself I was ready to relax. The teacher told us, in her softest and most reassuring voice, to 'let go', to 'surrender'. And I did ... for about three seconds, before the stream of thoughts began: *What am I doing here? Look at that girl's stomach. My wrists hurt. Do they have to talk so loudly outside? I cannot believe she said that today! How am I supposed to relax when all this is happening? What should I make for dinner? Is it going to rain tomorrow?*

Then I got a dog. A great big 55 kg Bernese Mountain Dog of a dog named Forest. A living, breathing, furry distraction. And sure, with his huge paws and brown eyes, he was a balm for the soul. I joked (half-joked) that he was my therapy dog. Forey did bring enormous joy and love into our lives, but the bee still buzzed. Relentlessly.

About the same time, Tom was travelling a lot for work, which meant I often had the weekends to myself. I didn't mind, as my year in Italy had taught me how to enjoy time on my own. Unfortunately though, now it had become less a case of wanting to stay in than needing to. Going out was just too hard.

On one particular Saturday night, following a grey, unremarkable day, I felt compelled to lose myself in a task. I wanted to feel the magic that comes with the process of making something simple. So, for the first time in many years, I decided to make pasta. I poured myself a glass of wine, turned on some Frank Sinatra and started to knead.

The eggs and flour gradually became a bright yellow dough that I squished, rolled and folded to the sounds of 'That's Life'. It felt oddly satisfying to channel the unadulterated anger of another horrible, demoralising week into the pasta dough. I wrapped up the dough, set it aside to rest and started to make a basic tomato sauce that would require very little from me. Moving around the kitchen with no distractions, I felt at ease. There was no pressure to make this perfect (something, I realised, I expected far too often). Here I was, cooking purely for my own pleasure.

I ran the dough through the pasta machine over and over again, until I had long, smooth, pliable sheets that flapped as I fed them through. I cut them into ribbons and then plunged the pasta into a saucepan of rapidly boiling salty water, watching as fat bubbles made their way from the bottom of the pan to burst at the surface. After a few minutes, I pulled out the tagliatelle and flung the long strands directly into the sauce, making a mess. I tossed everything together, listening closely to the sounds of the pasta embracing the deep red sauce, and finished it off with a drizzle of olive oil and a heavy snowfall of Parmigiano Reggiano. I stood in my kitchen, eating it straight from the pan. Making something from scratch and enjoying it proved to be a reaffirming, soul-restoring experience. It gave me a new brightness that made the dirty T-shirt I wore seem almost clean. It felt good. I had switched off. I was calm.

I enjoyed it so much that I repeated the exercise the following Saturday night, and then again the following weekend. This grounding routine quickly became addictive. I started keeping my Saturday nights free for pasta making and groaned whenever something else would inconveniently crop up.

Missing out on my Saturday night pasta ritual made me feel unexpectedly glum.

When I shared my newfound enthusiasm with friends, they often couldn't understand why I would go to so much effort, especially when I was cooking mostly for myself. But rather than feeling lonely or sad, it made me feel valued and present. I found cooking in private to be intensely therapeutic. It was pure pleasure. My weeks suddenly became filled with pasta planning. I would carry around my Saturday night pasta ideas all week, tucked safely in my pocket. Saturday mornings were spent at the markets, picking up supplies, or at home playing a game of 'raid the pantry for a pasta sauce' – which yielded many delicious rewards. Come Saturday evening, I'd settle on my pasta shape of choice, pour myself a glass of wine and dip into a playlist of old favourites by Frank, Dean, Ella and Louis. I wasn't trying to cook like a professional or impress anyone, but none of my pastas ever felt like a failure. Rather, I'd learn from my mistakes and become even more curious, which drove me to do more research, planning and, most importantly, try more pasta. And all these things made me happy.

Gradually, my new ritual restored in me a sense of balance; it offered me an interest, a hobby, something else to think about. It showed me that there were many facets to my identity, and that it was important to embrace and derive value from all of them. Most of all, it taught me mindfulness: I learned to focus on the process rather than the result. It was a decidedly pleasant bonus that the result just so happened to be a delicious and rewarding one. It nourished me, it gave me the energy to fight the good fight, and the tools to tackle anxiety when I felt it creeping in.

M.F.K Fisher, arguably the world's best food writer, once said, 'No yoga exercise, no meditation in a chapel filled with music will rid you of your blues better than the humble task of making your own bread.' For me, it is the act of making pasta – be it kneading the dough or the comforting sound of dried rigatoni being tipped into bubbling water – that has healing powers beyond anything that I can quantify.

This is not a dramatic tale of overcoming incredible adversity or surviving some kind of disaster. No loves have been lost, no hearts broken. This is a rather ordinary tale, my tale, of finding oneself through the love of making pasta, and the journey of forming a ritual of self-care that I like to call Saturday Night Pasta.

FIVE THINGS I'VE LEARNED
FROM MAKING PASTA

1

Pasta waits for no one. Just like life,
it should be enjoyed in the moment.

2

Making pasta deserves your attention.
It needs to be 'kneaded' and it should be cooked
with the same amount of love and attention.

3

The best pastas are the simplest.
Don't overcomplicate or overthink them.

4

Always salt your water like you live your life,
with abundance.

5

Sometimes the missing ingredient is right
there in front of you ... even a little of the
cooking water can magically transform
a sauce into something extraordinary.

SATURDAY NIGHT PASTA GUIDE

Pastatation

'past-a-tay-tion'

noun

1. The action or practice of meditating through making pasta. 'She practises pastatation every Saturday night.'

2. A discourse intended to express its author's reflections or to guide others in contemplation. 'She uses pastatation as a way of becoming relaxed and calm.'

synonyms

meditation, mindfulness, contemplation, reflection, yoga

To really understand the power of Saturday Night Pasta, I recommend trying this first by yourself – or at least with someone who loves you just the way you are. For me, learning to make pasta alone felt safe. It became a place to learn, to make mistakes and know that the decisions I made were only going to affect what I ate and nothing beyond that. The absolute worst thing that could happen is that I would have a piece of toast for dinner. Naturally, fewer things go wrong when cooking for yourself because there just isn't as much riding on it. As a consequence, I built my confidence and learned to trust my instincts. I'm not a chef and I'm certainly not an expert in Italian food, I'm just a self-taught cook who delights in making pasta. And I think we've forgotten the importance of doing things solely because we enjoy them. What I find comforting about the process is that, even after a day when absolutely nothing is certain, I can come home and knead flour with eggs or water to make something magical. Sure, the pasta might not be perfect, but it means something because I made it with my own hands. That in itself makes it the best pasta in the world.

I suggest that you take notes along the way – soon you'll start to pick up nuances in the pasta and you'll be able to identify why this Saturday night's pasta was different from the last. Be self-forgiving, too. Failure is a reality of being human; accepting and learning from those failures will only make you a better cook.

Saturday is an obvious day to become absorbed in the kitchen. There's time to potter and just enjoy the rather alchemical task of making pasta. When you're young, staying home alone on a Saturday night can create fear. Labelled FOMO (Fear Of Missing Out), as I grew older it steadily became more like JOMO (Joy Of Missing Out). I began to feel rather smug sitting at home with a bowl of pasta and a glass of wine, watching the latest rom-com. I was surprised and comforted to realise that the only thing I got judged on was my movie choice.

I don't believe that you can't cook a dish just because it's only for yourself. That's the whole point of Saturday Night Pasta! Making the effort to cook something for yourself can only be a good thing, as it means you value yourself enough to put the energy and care into a meal simply because YOU feel like it. Cooking and eating alone can be one of the most empowering and pleasurable experiences we can have. So, if you feel like a lasagne then, goddamn, you should have that lasagne. Besides, not only does it make for the best leftovers, it freezes well, too.

Ironically, Saturday Night Pasta has turned into a social affair, with friends wanting to share in the pleasure of making pasta by hand. I won't deny that the act of cooking and eating connects people, so gathering friends around a table makes a rather lovely night in – although I recommend no more than three to ease the amount of dough making and avoid distraction with too much wine. I've had many memorable nights around my pasta bench, cooking, laughing and eating with friends. To watch people beam with pride while making their own pasta is like the endorphin release some say you get from exercise.

Then there's the satisfaction of cooking for friends. I enjoy nothing more than preparing for a dinner party, with pasta being the pièce de résistance. Sure, the alone time in the kitchen, just pottering and preparing the meal, is the therapy, but it feels good to delight friends with the homemade pasta you've spent the day making. Everybody loves pasta and I promise that even the simplest of sauces can result in the loudest admiration.

It's been reassuring to see others catch the Saturday Night Pasta bug, and feeling the same satisfaction and self-worth that it brought me. Connecting and sharing stories with people via Instagram is one of the really positive things that can come out of social media – and funny that food still has the power to connect, even though it's not sitting there in front of you. It fills me with an enormous sense of pride and fuzzy feelings when I see people indulging in a Saturday Night Pasta ritual and spreading that joy around the world. I really want to say it's more than just a night in because it feels bigger than that. So, I'm going to be bold and confident for once in my life and claim that it has, unintentionally might I add, become a movement.

Of course, you can't make pasta every night in the way some yogis practise every day. That would be unrealistic. But I do take great comfort in knowing that even on a Monday I'm only five days away from my ritual. Besides, that's why they invented dried pasta.

Setting the Saturday Night Pasta scene

SOLO SNP-ING

This is your time to be in the moment. A little moment you've carved out in your busy life to lose yourself in the task of making pasta. There should be no distractions. If you're like me and can easily be distracted by even a simple flicker of a light, then there are a few things I suggest you do to help set the scene and draw you into a little pasta-making bubble. This is my Saturday Night Pasta ritual.

- **Comfortable clothes.** While I'd like people to think I'm flouncing around in my red polka dot dress with a vintage white apron cinched around my waist, I'm more likely in a pair of exercise pants (this is a work-out after all) and an oversized shirt. Bra optional. Hair untamed.

- **Playlist.** I simply can't make pasta without the soothing sounds of Ella Fitzgerald, Louis Armstrong and Frank Sinatra on repeat. Tom tells me my playlist is more suited to a dining hall in a nursing home, but I can't describe the feeling that comes over me when I knead to Louis' gruff, throaty voice singing 'They can't take that away from me'. It makes me happy beyond words. If you, too, are soothed by the sounds of the 1950s, then you can find my Saturday Night Pasta Playlist on Spotify. But you might also knead to a different beat. Find what feeds you.

- **Put your phone on aeroplane mode.** I know it sounds harsh, but I seem to lack any self-control over picking up my phone and scrolling through Instagram. I've found myself dough deep and reaching for my phone for some Instagratification.

- **I always like to make and cook pasta with a glass of wine.** It makes me feel carefree and confident, almost sensual as I move around the kitchen. I think it's because when I lived in Italy, my Italian friend Andrea told me that it was criminal to cook without a glass of wine. So now in my pursuit to be an Italian domestic goddess, curves and all, I just can't go past it. Of course, that's just me, but pour yourself a soda with lemon or a cup of tea if you prefer. It's all part of the self-care.

- **Decide on what you're cooking.** Sometimes I will have spent the day planning; other days I live on the edge and decide right before I start based on what I have. Have your ingredients out on the bench to inspire you. A bowl of eggs, a plate of tomatoes, a vase of basil. I weigh out all my ingredients for the pasta. It feels methodical and organised. If you're following a recipe, read that through, too.

- **Don't forget to put your saucepan of water on to boil.** Large pans take a while to come to that rolling, lively boil you're after. Background bubbles bursting at the surface only add to the experience.

- **Take a deep breath.** Don't rush things. And remember this is all for just you. Little you. Reminding yourself of that point should allow you to shed any pressure and indulge in the pure pleasure of making pasta.

- **Sit at the table, lay a place mat out, light a candle, pour another drink.** You deserve it. Eat happily and wholeheartedly.

GROUP SNP-ING

Saturday Night Pasta with friends is based on the belief that kneading and laughter provides positive physiological and psychological benefits to the well-being of a person. It is usually done in groups, with eye contact, wine and lots of playfulness among participants.

This practice is a little different to solo SNP-ing. It's one where laughter and excitement take over. Yet it also brings a sense of togetherness. There should be no pressure. Instead, you are sharing in the thrill of making pasta with friends. Remember, your house is not a restaurant, so don't feel the need to make it one.

- **Do some prep ahead.** Whether that's making the sauce, chopping your ingredients, weighing out your flour or making a jug of negronis. Removing some of the steps ahead of time allows you to immerse yourself in the act of making pasta with friends and not worry about what else needs to be done.

- **Set the scene.** If you've got bowls stacked on the table, music going, ingredients out and a drink poured for yourself, it all adds to the laid-back vibe SNP requires. You want people to walk into a relaxed environment. Just like a yoga studio, but an SNP version.

- **Settle on a pasta shape that you think everyone can master.** Don't be too ambitious. You're not after perfect pasta shapes, but you do want guests to feel that satisfaction that comes from rolling a shape they can be proud of.

- **Friends who knead together, stay together.** Gather around your workbench and knead as a group. Use the resting time for a chat. Then roll out together. It's a hands-on kind of dinner party.

- **Give yourself time.** Unlike solo SNP-ing, you'll have distractions – usually in the form of a friend telling an engrossing story. Think about what you have to do and plan that out accordingly – for example, I always get everyone kneading straight away so the dough can rest. Otherwise you may end up eating too late. People get hungry and then they get hangry.

- **Put that saucepan of water on to boil while your friends make the pasta.**

- **When I have friends over, I like to have some things to nibble on when we are all kneading the dough to fend off any hunger pangs.** Something that requires no cooking: olives, cured meats, cheese etc. With the pasta, I serve little more than some bread and mixed leaves. Dessert is most likely a tub of store-bought vanilla ice cream served with either coffee, affogato style, or olive oil and salt.

- **Put your finished pasta on the table so everyone can help themselves.** It's a more relaxed form of dining. Chunks of Parmigiano Reggiano means everyone can grate over the cheese to their liking. Bottles of wine on the table allow everyone to drink at their own pace.

PASTA SCHOOL

Roald Dahl once said that, 'if you are interested in something, no matter what it is, go at it at full speed, embrace it with both arms, hug it, love it, and above all become passionate about it. Lukewarm is no good.'

About two years ago, my Saturday Night Pasta routine was in full flight. I had been practising for well over a year and decided that to take my hobby to the next level, I needed some formal training. For a now pasta obsessive, that formal training just had to be a short course in Italy.

Fast forward months of planning (and saving), I finally took myself to pasta school in Rome. Grano & Farina is a small professional cooking school run by a husband and wife team, chef Pino Ficara and sfoglina Julia Ficara. A sfoglina is a person who rolls out pasta by hand (very different to a machine). Purists consider this the only way to make pasta. Julia is an American who has lived in Italy for half her life (you'd be hard pressed to differentiate her Italian from a native speaker). She has dedicated herself to the art of handmade pasta, studying in Bologna as well as travelling around Italy learning from the best teachers, the Italian nonne.

I began an intensive four-day program covering pastas from the south, pastas from the north, four types of gnocchi and some pizza that was thrown in for good measure (we were in Italy, after all). The pièce de résistance, though, was learning from Julia how to roll out pasta by hand. I eagerly sat at the end of her bench and watched her work the dough, transforming it from a small ball into the most beautiful sheet of pasta that flapped in the breeze as she held it up. She had an innate understanding of the dough and knew how to gently handle any nuances that inevitably arose. There is a distinctive swoosh noise that is made when you roll out pasta by hand, like a cat's tongue licking you, and I wish I had recorded it for my sleep app.

Julia loves the art of la sfoglia so much that she competes every year in competitions that celebrate rolling out pasta by hand. I asked her how she goes, and she leant in to say under her breath, 'Well the judges can't exactly give the prize to an American over a 90-year-old nonna can they?', but that doesn't stop her from participating. It's the highlight of her summers.

Of course, I'm under no illusion that attending a short course in Italy makes me an expert – the Italian nonne prove that by having years of pasta making under their aprons – but what Julia and Pino gave me was a greater confidence with pasta that I hope, combined with my own humble discoveries, to pass on to you.

Pasta doughs

There are two main types of dough that I make for Saturday Night Pasta: a classic egg dough and a semolina dough. I add no salt or olive oil to my doughs. I was taught this by my Italian cooking teachers, who were firm on keeping the dough simple – and why bother complicating it? There is plenty of salt and oil to come.

EGG DOUGH

Egg pasta is undisputably renowned as Italy's best and is the dough most commonly made at home here in Australia. The basic dough consists of a soft wheat flour known as Tipo 00 and eggs. Watching this dough being rolled out by hand is a sight to behold. In Italy, there are competitions which celebrate the art of 'sfoglia' – the Italian word for rolling pasta by hand. Pasta rolled this way results in a texture and character that is impossible to achieve with a pasta machine. Of course, rolling by hand requires skill, experience and practice. This is a craft that takes years to master and is therefore the reason why a pasta machine has a place in my kitchen. Many purists will turn up their noses at a machine, but, for me, it opens up the wonderful world of homemade pasta. I've watched friends with no skill, bless them, make beautiful egg pasta on their very first go.

As with everything, there are lots of variations to making this pasta dough – from adding more egg yolks for a richer, brighter pasta, to adding ingredients, such as spinach or beetroot, for colour and flavour. I suggest mastering the basic egg dough ratio outlined on page 34 before experimenting with more yolks, as the more yolks you use the harder it is to knead the dough. The basic egg dough I use will also give you a good benchmark for comparing the texture with other doughs.

SEMOLINA DOUGH

This is the simplest dough you can make as it's just flour and water. However, it's the dough you're likely less familiar with. A lot of people are surprised to find out that pasta can be made without eggs and, in fact, most dried pasta on supermarket shelves is eggless. In Italy, you are more likely to find this type of pasta in the south, in the traditionally poorer parts of the country, where historically eggs were simply too expensive. There are hundreds of different shapes that can be made from this dough, mostly by hand, but it does require sourcing the right flour – semola di grano duro or semolina – made from hard wheat. While this flour is not as readily available as the classic soft wheat Tipo 00, it can be purchased from good Italian delicatessens and online.

I love this dough because irregularity is embraced – and let's hear it for irregularity; we need more of that in our lives. You can create shapes with it that look impressive, but in reality are very easy to make once you know how. Semolina dough is faster to make than egg dough and if you don't over-knead it, it doesn't need to rest. The dough won't be as stretchy as an egg dough, but it does have a surprisingly springy texture, which can give wonderful contrast to your finished dish. Finally, it doesn't need to be rolled out, making it the simplest of doughs to master.

Kneading pasta by hand

Kneading pasta by hand is an easy task that anyone can do. It's all about using your senses. You need to trust yourself here and really listen, watch and feel the dough. This is all part of the meditation of letting go and being present in the moment. Soon you will become accustomed to the feeling of the dough, its demand for more flour or moisture, when the gluten has stretched, and when the texture has changed – subtle as it might be. Food processors won't give you this.

As well as giving you a greater understanding of the dough, kneading by hand can help relieve the stress of the week for you. I can't emphasise enough the benefits of channelling a crappy week, a bad break-up, a broken heart or a frustrating conversation into the kneading of dough. At the end of a good knead, the dough will feel soft and silky and you will feel relaxed and satisfied. I don't think you can be bad at kneading either – it's really just pushing, squishing, squeezing and maybe a little rolling, all with a firm hand.

Even though the dough recipes follow a very basic formula, I always weigh my ingredients (digital scales help immensely) as it gives consistent results. Obviously the Italian nonne go by eyeball and adjust the amounts as needed, but they come with years of practice. Here's something I want to say up front: be aware that things like the humidity in the air, the size, age and water content of the eggs, and flour absorption rate can all play a role in your final dough, which might mean you need to add a splash of water or sprinkle of flour to your dough during the 'coming together' phase.

Egg dough requires more kneading than semolina dough due to the differences in gluten in the flours. Both doughs are made in the same way – the coming together of two ingredients, and then kneading to produce a beautiful dough ready to be made into pasta.

Form and position

I need to share a funny story. I was recently having an ultrasound on my abdomen and the doctor said to me, in all seriousness, 'You must do a lot of core exercise; you have the strongest abs!'. Tom nearly spat out his coffee. The truth of the matter is, my exercise routine is limited to my morning stroll with Tom and Forest to meet our neighbours for a coffee and perhaps, if I'm organised enough, one 40-minute Pilates class a fortnight. I have never had a strong core, I struggle to open a jar of capers and if you were to time me doing a body plank, I would barely make it to 20 seconds, but here the doctor was telling me how strong my muscles were. Her wrist was even getting sore as she pushed the ultrasound wand down. We laughed it off, Tom more so than me, may I add, and went on with our day. It wasn't until I was next making pasta that I realised I was holding and tightening my core as I kneaded the dough in and out. Would it be drawing a long bow to claim that pasta kneading is a physical exercise, as well as one of mental practice? I mean, by this stage I'd been making pasta almost every Saturday night for well over a year, so surely it's the sole reason I've developed these rock-hard abs?!

When I went to pasta school, form and position were two of the first things my teacher showed me. This is very important for Italian nonne – who are kneading and rolling out pasta all day, every day – to get right or they risk the development of arthritic pain. I mean, it's impressive to watch an 85-year-old nonna roll out pasta dough by hand with such gusto. Obviously, form and position are even more important to master if you are rolling out pasta by hand. So, armed with this knowledge and my newfound abs of steel, I present my pasta workout.

PASTA WORKOUT

- Plant your feet hip-width apart, making sure you are putting even weight on both feet. Keep your knees slightly bent, you don't want to lock them.

- Take a deep breath, roll your shoulders back and drop down your back. You don't want to be kneading with your shoulders up by your ears.

- Tilt forward from your hips, not your back, and start kneading the dough. Pull in your belly button (imagining that you are holding a blueberry in there) and start to knead. The power should be coming from your core, not your arms. Release your core as you exhale and tighten as you inhale.

- You might find that it is more comfortable to put one leg forward for more strength. If this is the case, position your leading leg forward and push the weight through it as you knead forward, then push the weight back on the other leg as you bring the dough back, in keeping with your breathing.

- After one knead, make sure to roll your shoulders back again to reset. Take a sip of wine for hydration and continue.

Basic egg dough

The recipe for a basic egg dough is universal and follows the ratio of one to one – that's one egg to 100 g (⅔ cup) of flour per person. However, for consistent results, egg dough requires 55 per cent hydration, so while we say 1 egg, you're looking for a cracked egg weight of 55 g. I'll add that this is a pretty standard weight for an egg; just avoid those jumbo eggs! A digital set of scales will sort you out. If your egg is slightly heavier, just scoop out some white with the shell; if it's too light, add a splash of water. Always weigh your eggs in a separate bowl before adding to the flour.

More often than not I'm making pasta just for myself, or for me and my husband, so I simply use 200 g (1⅓ cups) of Tipo 00 flour and two eggs (110 g). I wouldn't bother making pasta for any less as it's too difficult to knead. To feed more mouths, just increase the ratio. So, to make pasta for four people, use 400 g (2⅔ cups) of Tipo 00 flour and four eggs (220 g). I find the ideal size of dough to knead is for four to six people. Any more and it becomes a bigger challenge (but totally possible; just make sure you master that form and position).

I like to make my pasta directly on a wooden pasta bench; it makes me feel all romantic and Italian about the process. Wiser people will start it off in a big bowl, so they don't have to spend the time cleaning and scraping the dough off the bench.

Egg dough will keep in the fridge tightly wrapped in plastic wrap for up to two days. Be warned that it might discolour slightly. Always bring your dough to room temperature before you roll.

Serves 2

200 g (1⅓ cups) Tipo 00 flour, plus extra for dusting
2 × 55 g eggs at room temperature

Weigh out your flour and place it in a bowl or on a clean work surface. Make a well in the middle of the flour and pour in your eggs. Using a fork, whisk the eggs. Once the eggs are combined, slowly incorporate the flour from the top of the well, bringing more flour in as you work your way around the inner edge of the well. Take a deep breath as you do this, and breathe out as you hit 12 o'clock in the movement of your rotation. Repeat this circular movement a few more times until you have clumps of dough. You'll now have the urge to use your hands; succumb to that urge. If you have used a bowl, turn the dough out onto a clean, dry work surface. Squeeze the dough together with both hands, turning the dough as you do this to continue bringing the ingredients together. It's important to take a mental note of the texture here, as it will serve as a reminder later on as to how far you've taken the dough. Watching and feeling the dough change is a small, satisfying step in realising your contribution to the alchemy of eggs and flour. Keep squeezing, turning and slowly kneading the dough together.

If the air is very dry (hello air-conditioning or an open window nearby) or if your eggs were too small, your dough might be too dry. If this is the case, a spray bottle of water comes in handy to evenly mist the dough. That being said, if you lightly wet your hands and continue to knead it will do a similar job. If you're finding that your dough is very sticky, however, then maybe your eggs were too big. Here, a light dusting of flour will do the trick, bringing the dough into what I like to call 'neutral', where it feels just right.

Feel the need to knead. Form the dough into a ball, then, using the heel of one hand press down and push the dough forward to form an oval shape. Wrap your fingers around the top of the dough and then pull the dough back towards you. Channel the stress and worry in the back of your shoulders down into the dough. Continue in this manner, pushing out with the heel of your hand and drawing in with your fingers. Out, in. Out, in. You'll notice that the flour continues to absorb more of the egg and that the texture begins to change. Things become more elastic, soft and springy. Don't forget to breathe.

All in all, knead the dough for 8–10 minutes. The 'done' indicator is when you gently press into the dough with your finger and it springs back. It should be smooth and silky. Form the dough back into a ball, then wrap it in plastic wrap and press it down to form a disk. Set aside for 30 minutes for the dough to relax, which makes it easier to roll out through a pasta machine or by hand. This is also your opportunity to take a time out. The beauty in the humble act of making pasta is that you, too, should slow down.

Many recipes call for the dough to rest in the fridge. I prefer to rest it at room temperature for up to an hour, away from direct sunlight, as I find it makes the dough easier to roll out.

Rolling egg dough

BY MACHINE

Okay, it's time to roll out your dough. A pasta machine is a sure-fire way to make beautiful pasta at home on your very first go. As I only have a small machine, which I assume you do, too, I cut the dough in half (or thirds or quarters depending on how much dough I've made) to make it more manageable. Wrap any dough you aren't rolling back in plastic wrap or a tea towel to ensure that it doesn't dry out.

Set the pasta machine to the widest setting. Roll the dough through the machine once, then fold the dough in half and flatten with your hands or a rolling pin. Turn the dough 90 degrees and send it back through.

Press lightly on the dough to eliminate any air bubbles – a firm roll with a rolling pin or a bottle of wine helps, rather like a steamroller. Repeat twice, folding and turning the dough each time before rolling it through the machine again. Roll it through once more, but this time do not fold it – just feed the dough through the machine, giving it a gentle pull to create a long and regular shape. You are now ready to thin out your pasta sheet.

Turn the dial on your pasta machine up to the next number, to reduce the gap between the rollers. Feed the dough in and help pull it through as you turn the handle. It may be easier to have someone help you do this on your first go, as the dough can get unwieldy, but I promise that you will get the hang of it pretty quickly. The thing to remember is to continue turning halfway through. You can reverse if necessary, but otherwise keep rolling the dough through and maintain the pace. Continue to feed the dough through, each time turning the dial to reduce the size of the gap between the rollers. If your dough starts to look a little sticky, lightly dust with flour before continuing. The pasta will get very long – again, I sometimes find it too much to handle so I cut it in half, ensuring that I cover the half I'm not using with a tea towel or plastic wrap. Keep reducing the setting and

feeding the dough through, stretching and thinning the pasta until you have reached your desired thickness (see page 52).

BY HAND

As we have already discussed, there is an art to rolling out egg dough by hand; however, don't let that stop you giving it a go. While I am no expert on hand rolling, what I am is an advocate for giving homemade pasta a go, machine or no machine. A large, lightly floured bench and rolling pin (or a bottle of wine if you're desperate) are all you need to get started and produce pasta. The turning and rolling of the dough apply here too, so you will want to keep rotating the dough as you roll it out to your desired thickness. Julia, my pasta teacher, uses a clock analogy: turn from 12-2-4-6-8-10 but no more. Always roll away from you with even pressure. To make it more manageable as a beginner (and if you are short on space), I'd suggest cutting the dough up and rolling out in batches (purists, look away). When you've reached your desired thickness, roll your pin over the dough with no pressure to even it out. Rolling by hand is hard work, but with a little practice and experience, you will be producing beautiful, even sheets of pasta.

CURING YOUR PASTA

Most egg pasta should be 'cured' before being cut into the desired shape. This simply means to let it dry for 5–10 minutes, flipping the dough over halfway through, until it's starting to dry but not cracking. This will help you to cut the dough without it sticking together, especially if you're using a machine to cut the ribbons. The curing time will depend on the weather, air flow, whether or not you machine rolled or hand rolled, and your desired shape, so keep a close eye on it. The exception is filled pasta, which is best made straight away, taking advantage of the soft, moist dough.

EGG PASTA MANTRA

Weigh ingredients

Make well in flour

Add eggs and whisk

Gradually add flour with fork

Eventually add all flour with hands

Knead by hand for 10 minutes

Wrap in plastic wrap

Leave to rest for 30 minutes

Breathe

Roll out dough

Cut into desired shape

Plunge into boiling water as salty as sea

Cook until al dente

Keep some pasta cooking water

Toss pasta together with sauce

Eat

Basic semolina dough

Semolina pasta works with the same quantities of flour per person as egg pasta, so 100 g (⅔ cup) semolina flour for one person. The ideal moisture content, however, is slightly lower and you'll require 45 ml of water per 100 g of flour. So, for two people, you're looking at 200 g (1⅓ cups) semolina flour to 90 ml of warm water. For four, it will be 400 g (2⅔ cups) of flour to 180 ml of warm water. The dough can be kept in the fridge, tightly wrapped in plastic wrap, for up to two days. Always bring your dough to room temperature before using.

Serves 2

200 g (1⅓ cups) semola di grano duro (semolina), plus extra for dusting
90 ml warm water

Here I am wiser and use a bowl, otherwise the water will run everywhere. Weigh out your ingredients and place the flour in a large shallow bowl. Using your fingers, make a well in the middle of the flour and pour in the warm water. Use your hands to mix the water and flour. Once things have started to come together, you can tip the dough onto your work surface. You'll still have small bits of flour everywhere and the texture will be very crumbly. Take a deep breath and squeeze everything together, moving the dough around with force to mop up any excess flour. A pastry cutter helps to cut the dough to reveal the wetter parts, which can then be used to mop up any remaining flour. Now we knead.

If you've already made egg pasta dough, you'll notice that the semolina dough has a different texture and touch. It won't be as stretchy and pillowy as an egg dough, but the end result will still be silky and smooth. Squeeze your dough into a ball. Cup your hands around the dough and, using your palms, push the dough out, wrap your fingers around the top and roll it back in. Think of it as a tide going in and out, in and out. You don't want to be tearing the dough apart, but using the stretch to push it forward and roll it back up. You may find it easier to push with the heel of one hand and roll the dough back up on itself with your other hand. Remember to breathe. Even though we are unwinding here, we still want to keep moving at an energetic pace to prevent the dough from drying out. Like egg dough, if things start to feel too dry, mist or wet your hands and continue to knead. Keep kneading the dough for 5–7 minutes, no more. You'll notice the texture change substantially – it will become smooth and soft, just like a baby's bottom! Wrap in plastic wrap or a tea towel and leave to rest for 20 minutes. Breathe. Nice job.

SEMOLINA PASTA MANTRA

Weigh ingredients

Make well in flour

Pour in warm water

Combine with hands

Tip onto clean surface

Squeeze together

Move dough around to mop up flour

Knead by hand for 5 minutes

Wrap in plastic wrap

Leave to rest for 20 minutes

Breathe

Cut and roll into desired shape

Plunge into boiling water as salty as sea

Cook until al dente

Keep some pasta cooking water

Toss pasta together with sauce

Eat

Pasta Shapes

These are the shapes I make most often for Saturday Night Pasta. Split into egg dough and semolina dough, the exercises are easy to master in a few simple steps and require very little equipment.

Before we get started

A NOTE ON SHAPE

Some pasta shapes are simple to make; others are tricky and will take some practice. Some shapes require certain equipment and then there are those that are best left to the professionals or commercial extruders.

On the following pages, I have chosen the pasta shapes that I make most often. They are achievable, satisfying and unlikely to put you in a bad place mentally (and trust me, I can tell you from experience there is nothing that gets you more worked up than following someone on YouTube making things look so easy with a simple twist of the fingers; meanwhile, all you've created is a soggy strand of pasta that has started to melt from the heat of your fingers). Saturday Night Pasta is about soothing you, creating a Zen environment for you to relax and surrender to. I don't want to find you lying on the floor kicking and screaming.

I've included the basics, but also some lesser-known shapes that you'll be quietly chuffed you've made with your own two hands. These shapes seem to delight people. I think that because they aren't shapes you see everywhere they do look impressive, but I know (and soon you will, too) that they are very easily mastered.

I've settled on only two filled pastas in this book, mainly because I find that folding filled pasta can really stress people out, but I encourage you to master these two shapes and then move on to more challenges. To really nail filled pasta, you are better off watching videos online or being shown how to make it. It is truly hard to break it down into steps without confusing the reader. I am quite comfortable making filled pasta, but I can still get flustered when reading some recipes – *put this finger there, then your index finger over there, then roll it up using a swift flick of the thumb.* I can assure you that a simple tagliatelle or cavatelli/malloreddus is equally as satisfying to make.

You'll also notice that I've left out gnocchi. I adore gnocchi and once mastered it is a joy to make, however, quite simply, there is more scope for things to go wrong. It's bitterly disappointing to get to the end of all that effort to find you've made gummy gnocchi thanks to a simple extra knead of the dough.

This isn't meant to be your one-stop pasta book. Once you've caught the pasta-making bug, I highly recommend you go out and buy some books that will take you even further (see my recommendations on page 201).

A NOTE ON FORM

You'll see in the following pages that my pasta shapes aren't perfect. As much as I try to cut a square that's precisely measured on each side, it's never exact. My ravioli never meets perfectly and my busiate lengths are never the same. I've never been able to cut a straight line (hell, I even struggle to walk in a straight line – be warned if you're walking next to me, it's almost guaranteed that I'll walk into you). My point is that while I try to keep things as measured as I can, I don't sweat the imperfections. Irregularity should be embraced in the home kitchen. The same goes with the thickness and length of my pasta. There are guidelines in Italy, but I find myself making slightly thicker or odd-length versions due to my skill level, patience or desire for a better bite. While I don't strive for perfection, I do try for consistency once I get rolling. This just helps when it comes to cooking the pasta.

Like everything in this book, there are lots of different ways to create the pasta shapes listed here; just go online and check out the multiple videos by nonne, chefs and other home cooks, but as Julia my pasta teacher told me, if a particular method works for you, then do it that way.

Egg dough exercises

All of these pasta exercises require the dough to be rolled out. The long pasta shapes pretty much follow the same steps, but are cut at slightly different widths. The last three shapes – farfalle, garganelli and paccheri – require a few more steps. Remember to keep your rolled-out dough covered in plastic wrap or a tea towel to stop it drying out.

Egg dough pasta shapes

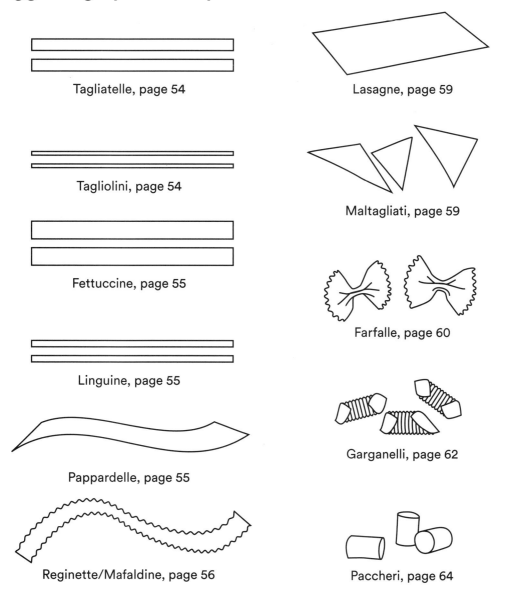

Tagliatelle, page 54

Tagliolini, page 54

Fettuccine, page 55

Linguine, page 55

Pappardelle, page 55

Reginette/Mafaldine, page 56

Lasagne, page 59

Maltagliati, page 59

Farfalle, page 60

Garganelli, page 62

Paccheri, page 64

51

Thickness guide

Pasta machines vary in setting sizes, so here I've given millimetre measurements for those hand rolling, as well as indicating the thickness that each setting approximately gives.

0 setting on a machine – or the thickest – is what you run your dough through a couple of times to start. Once you're happy with the dough in feel and shape, you're ready to roll. You should only feed the sheet through once for the remaining settings, although if you do make a mistake and end up with air bubbles or a wonky sheet, feel free to run it through the same setting to smooth things out.

0) **4.8 mm** roll your dough through a few times

1) **3.8 mm** keep it rollin'

2) **3.3 mm** keep it rollin'

3) **2.5 mm** keep it rollin'

4) **1.9 mm** yep, keep going

5) **1.5 mm** I like my garganelli, paccheri, pappardelle, and reginette/mafaldine at this thickness.

6) **1.2 mm** farfalle, fettuccine, lasagne, linguine

7) **1 mm** Here is where I take agnolotti, ravioli, tagliatelle and tagliolini.

8) **0.8 mm** I rarely venture this thin, as I find the dough is hard to navigate through the machine, plus I tend to like my pasta with more bite. But for purists, this is ideal for tagliatelle and tagliolini.

9) **0.6 mm** Roll if you dare. I don't bother.

Cutting long pasta

Like all pasta shapes in Italy, long egg pastas have set widths, lengths and thicknesses. These 'set' measurements can vary between region, town and family. The following pages show the widths and thicknesses I hand-cut tagliatelle, tagliolini, fettucine, linguine, pappardelle and reginette/mafaldine, but to be completely frank, I often find myself making a mix of them all due to my unsteady hand, even if I have my trusty ruler handy. I just don't know how the nonne cut them so perfectly! This unevenness often leads me to the cutting accessories on my pasta machine – I have tagliatelle, tagliolini and linguine attachments that click on and cut my pasta sheets perfectly each time. As fettuccine and pappardelle are wider, I cut these by hand and then celebrate the irregularities I produce.

I certainly don't worry about the lengths of the strands, just that they are roughly the same, which is normally determined by the length I roll my pasta sheet.

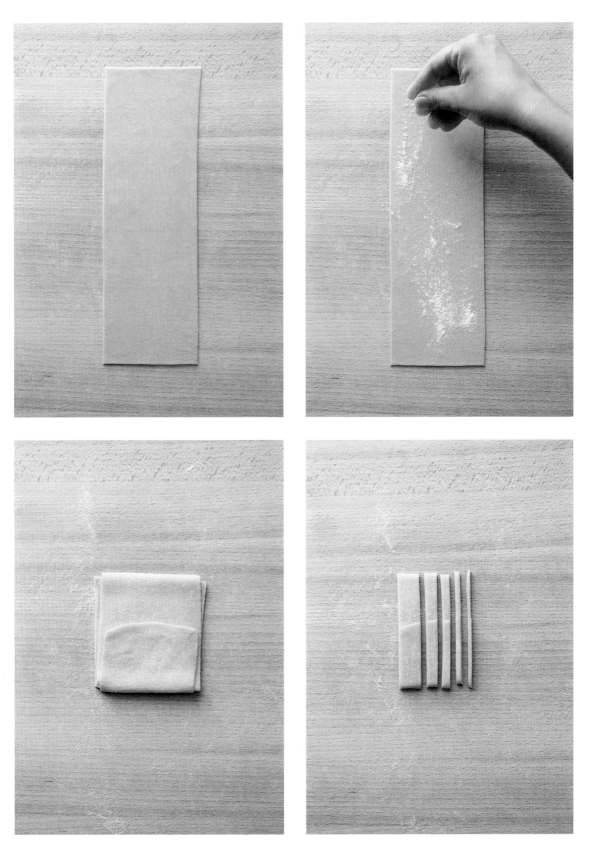

Tagliatelle and tagliolini

Arguably Italy's most highly regarded pasta, tagliatelle comes from the word 'tagliare', which means 'to cut' (tagliolini is the thinner version of tagliatelle). This pasta shape can be found all over Italy, although the birthplace is considered to be Emilia-Romagna, where inspiration was supposedly taken from the long blonde hair of a royal bride. In Emilia-Romagna there are strict guidelines on the size, width and thickness of tagliatelle (the pasta sheet's thickness is tested by holding it up against a window to ensure you can see through it). Of course, I break all the rules here – I use my machine to cut the strands and keep them slightly thicker, as I just prefer that added bite. Purists would argue this is not tagliatelle, but for you, me and anyone else who isn't bound by tradition, I'm going to call it tagliatelle or tagliolini.

If you have a tagliatelle and/or tagliolini attachment on your pasta machine, simply feed your pasta sheet through the rollers after letting the pasta 'cure' for 5 minutes if necessary (a wet sheet will be hard to cut and the strands will stick together; see page 38). If you don't have one of these attachments, follow the instructions above right.

Equipment: n/a

Level: easy

Make your desired quantity of egg pasta dough following the recipe on page 34.

- Roll your dough as thinly as you dare. For me, this is around 1 mm thick.

- If your dough is sticky, leave the sheet to slightly 'cure' for 5 minutes.

- Lightly flour your sheet, then gently fold it up.

- Using a knife, cut the sheet into ribbons.
  – For tagliatelle, cut 8 mm-wide strips
  – For tagliolini, cut 2 mm-wide strips

- Unravel the pasta sheet to release the ribbons.

You can then hang your pasta ribbons over the back of a chair, on a coat hanger or anywhere you can. I have a little pasta-drying stand. You can also curl the pasta into nests and keep on a well-floured surface.

Fettuccine and linguine

Fettuccine literally means 'ribbons'. Originating from Rome, it is the central Italian version of tagliatelle. Fettuccine is slightly thicker than its northern sister, and it's probably the shape you are more used to seeing, as it's more commonly found in dried form on supermarket shelves.

Also found on all supermarket shelves, linguine shares a similar thickness to fettuccine but the individual strands are much thinner. The name translates to 'little tongues' because the shape of the long noodle is meant to be curved rather than flat, just like your tongue. It's a shape typically found in Genoese cuisine and is often served with seafood or pesto.

Equipment: n/a

Level: easy

Make your desired quantity of egg pasta dough following the recipe on page 34.

- Roll your dough until it is 1.2 mm thick.

- If your dough is sticky, leave the sheet to slightly 'cure' for 5 minutes.

- Lightly flour your sheet, then gently fold it up.

- Using a knife, cut the sheet into ribbons.
  – For fettuccine, cut 1–1.2-cm wide ribbons
  – For linguine, cut 4 mm-wide strips

- Unravel the pasta sheet to release the ribbons.

You can then hang your pasta ribbons over the back of a chair, on a coat hanger or anywhere you can. I have a little pasta-drying stand. You can also curl the pasta into nests and keep on a well-floured surface.

Pappardelle

These thick and slippery pasta ribbons are a crowd favourite, perfect for the rich and gamey ragùs of Tuscany. In Tuscan dialect, pappardelle stems from the word 'pappare' meaning 'to eat' or 'gobble', and this certainly suits the thick sauces it is served with. I love the slopping sound when you toss thick pappardelle through a hearty stew. It screams winter comfort.

Equipment: n/a

Level: easy

Make your desired quantity of egg pasta dough following the recipe on page 34.

- Roll your dough until it is 1.5 mm thick.

- If your dough is sticky, leave the sheet to slightly 'cure' for 5 minutes.

- Lightly flour your sheet, then gently fold it up.

- Using a knife, cut the sheet into 2–2.5 cm-wide ribbons.

- Unravel the pasta sheet to release the ribbons.

You can then hang your pasta ribbons over the back of a chair, on a coat hanger or anywhere you can. I have a little pasta-drying stand. You can also curl the pasta into nests and keep on a well-floured surface.

Reginette/Mafaldine

I find cutting reginette (also called mafaldine) with a fluted pastry cutter intensely therapeutic. There's something about the resistance of the wheel against the soft dough, which leaves a pretty, ruffled cut. While the edges do serve a practical purpose by collecting the sauce, they also represent the crowns worn by queens and princesses (reginette means 'little queens'). The shape was created to celebrate the birth of Princess Mafalda (born to the last King of Italy). There is something so delightful about this shape, which works well with a variety of sauces, but particularly a loose ragù.

Equipment: fluted pastry cutter

Level: easy

Make your desired quantity of egg pasta dough following the recipe on page 34.

- Roll your dough until it is 1.5 mm thick.
- If your dough is sticky, leave the sheet to slightly 'cure' for 5 minutes.
- Lightly flour your sheet, then gently fold it up.
- Using a fluted pastry wheel, cut the sheet into 1.5–2 cm-wide ribbons.
- Unravel the pasta sheet to release the ribbons.

You can then hang your pasta ribbons over the back of a chair, on a coat hanger or anywhere you can. I have a little pasta-drying stand. You can also curl the pasta into nests and keep on a well-floured surface.

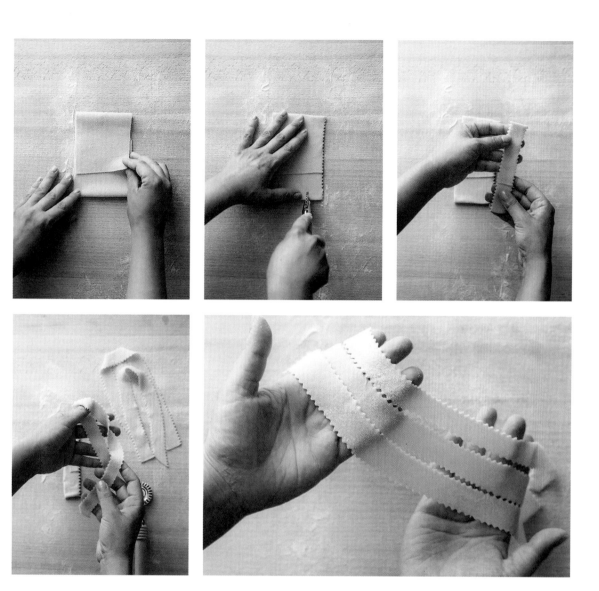

Lasagne

Lasagna (the plural being lasagne) is the wide pasta sheet that is layered to create the baked pasta dish of the same name – lasagne al forno. Lasagna is actually one of the oldest Italian pasta shapes, with the name cited in historical texts dating back well before the 13th century. It ranges from a square of pasta to wide strips, and its thickness varies throughout Italy. In Bologna, spinach is sometimes added to the dough, while in the south it can be made without eggs. It's meant to be rolled very thinly, even thinner than tagliatelle, but I prefer to keep it on the thicker side because I double-cook it.

Equipment: n/a

Level: easy

Make your desired quantity of egg pasta dough following the recipe on page 34.

- Roll your dough to about 1.2 mm thick.
- Cut the sheets to fit your chosen baking dish.
- Cover with tea towels to stop the pasta drying out, until you are ready to plunge the sheets (three to five at a time, depending on the size of your pot) into boiling salted water for 30 seconds before assembling your lasagne.

Maltagliati

Translating to 'badly cut', this is a brilliant shape for hiding pasta mistakes. Nothing goes to waste in Italy, so originally maltagliati were the left-over scraps from making tagliatelle. I collect my pasta scraps, cut them into rough shapes and leave them to dry, then after a few Saturday nights I end up with enough for them to star in their own mid-week pasta dish. The shape has taken on a range of different names all over Italy – my favourite is 'malmaritati', which translates to 'badly married'.

Equipment: n/a

Level: easy

Instructions for this shape couldn't be easier. Simply cut your left-over pasta into 4–6 cm rough strips, squares or diamonds.

Farfalle

The word 'farfalle' means 'butterflies'. The size can vary depending on who is making them and how precise they want to be. The shape is found throughout Italy, although it might be called something different depending on where you are. I like to cut mine with a fluted pastry cutter so they look pretty, but you can, of course, cut them with a straight edge.

Equipment: fluted pastry cutter, ruler

Level: easy

Make your desired quantity of egg pasta dough following the recipe on page 34.

- Roll your dough until it is 1.2 mm thick.

- Cut your sheet into 4 cm x 3 cm-wide rectangles (although the size is really up to you; just keep them in a ratio of chubby rectangles). I use a fluted pastry cutter here to get those lovely crimped edges.

- Lay out the pasta rectangles with one of the longer sides facing you.

- Position your thumb at the base of one pasta rectangle, then place your index finger in the middle and your middle finger at the top. Using your thumb and middle finger, gently squeeze the top and bottom of the rectangle towards the centre to form a butterfly or bowtie shape. Voila! Your middle finger should have created a little crevice to allow for even cooking.

- Repeat and leave to dry for about 15 minutes before cooking.

Garganelli

Hailing from Emilia-Romagna, garganelli's thin ridged tubes are meant to look like the oesophagus of a chicken (which translates to 'garganel', hence the name garganelli). According to folklore, a poor nonna in the hills of Emilia-Romagna had cut the pasta into squares ready to fold tortellini, only to find that her cat had eaten all the filling. With her family hungry and ready for dinner, she thought on her feet (like all good thrifty nonne do) and rolled the pasta squares over a basket to create garganelli's ridged shape.

This shape does require a gnocchi board and a dowel, but if you don't have a dowel hanging around (I don't), then use the end of a wooden spoon. Garganelli are very easy to make and the process will give you a spritely spring in your step.

Equipment: gnocchi board, ruler, dowel or wooden spoon

Level: easy–medium

Make your desired quantity of egg pasta dough following the recipe on page 34.

- Roll your dough until it is 1.5 mm thick.

- Cut your sheet into 4 cm squares. I recommend using a ruler here, as the more exact your squares are, the easier they are to match and roll.

- Leave the squares to slightly 'cure' for 5 minutes, as this helps the garganelli keep their hollow shape.

- Flour your gnocchi board – and keep it well floured throughout the process – you don't want your garganelli to stick.

- Position a pasta square in a diamond shape in front of you on your gnocchi board.

- Wrap the bottom point over and around a dowel or the handle of a wooden spoon, pressing down as you roll.

- Roll the dowel or spoon forward to seal the points together, using the gnocchi board to create a ridged pattern.

- Carefully remove the garganelli and repeat.

- Leave for 15 minutes to dry out before cooking to help retain their shape.

63

Paccheri

This is one of my favourite pasta shapes. Originally hailing from Campania – and now one of the most popular pasta shapes in Naples – paccheri (say it with me – 'pak-keri') are thick, large tubes that are thought to resemble squid tubes. Sometimes I cut the tubes in half to make 'calamari' or calamarata, which is the shape I like to serve with my calamari ragù (see page 146).

There are many tales about the origin of this pasta. The word is thought to mean 'slap' in Neapolitan dialect, representing the sound made when the pasta is gobbled up. A more colourful legend, however, is one that involves corruption and deceit. It has been said that the shape was created to smuggle banned garlic cloves across the alps into what was then Prussia. Apparently Italian garlic was superior, and because of this the Prussian government banned it in order to keep local farmers afloat. The garlic-smuggling operation was so successful that eventually the Prussian industry folded.

There are several ways to make paccheri. For true authenticity, you will need to use a thick dowel, but I prefer the more 'homely' approach of simply rolling a rectangle and pushing down to seal. A swift trim of the ends then squares it up. If you do have a suitable-sized dowel, you can roll the pasta on a gnocchi board to create ridges, which would then make this a handmade rigatoni. You do want to keep the pasta reasonably thick to help the tubes retain their shape. And your dough should be on the drier side so the tubes don't cave in.

Equipment: ruler, knife
(I use a pizza cutter to trim)

Level: easy–medium

Make your desired quantity of egg pasta dough following the recipe on page 34.

- Roll your dough until it is 1.5 mm thick.

- Using a ruler, cut your sheet into 7 cm x 4–4.5 cm rectangles.

- Leave the rectangles to slightly 'cure' for 5 minutes.

- Working with one rectangle at a time, bring the short sides together, roughly overlapping them by 1 cm, to form a tube, then press down to seal. A very small run of a wet finger down the edge can help seal the tube if you're having difficulties.

- Continue pressing the seal until it is the same thickness as the rest of the tube. I put my finger inside the tube and press along the seam to help.

- If you like, trim the edges of the tube to neaten it up and help the tube stand up.

- Stand the tube upright on a well-floured surface and leave to dry for 20–30 minutes. This will help to hold its shape when cooking. The longer you leave them to dry out, the more likely they will keep their shape.

- Repeat with the remaining rectangles.

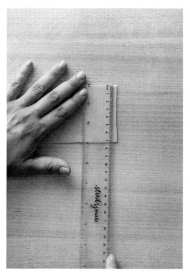

Semolina dough exercises

The great thing about the pasta shapes below is that they are all made by hand, so rightly celebrate irregularity. No pasta machine needed here. You don't need to stress too much about getting your pasta shapes perfect. Like all things, practice helps. If you're finding the dough is hard to roll out, you're either applying too much pressure or you need to give your dough a rest. There is no need to dry your semolina pasta shapes, but there is no harm in letting them dry either. If you'd like to make your shapes ahead of time, you can simply leave them uncovered on a clean, dry tea towel or mesh drying rack.

Semolina pasta shapes

Pici, page 69

Orecchiette, page 77

Busiate, page 70

Strozzapreti, page 78

Cavatelli/Malloreddus, page 73

Fregola, page 80

Maccheroni a descita, page 74

Pici

Originating from southern Tuscany, these handmade noodles, which vary in width and length according to the hands that make them, embrace irregularity. Pici was known as a poor folks' dish, served alongside a rustic garlic sauce and breadcrumbs. Those who could afford more enjoyed it with duck, boar or mushroom ragù. While it's as simple as rolling a sausage of dough into long, thin and uneven noodles, it does take some practice to get into the rhythm of the roll. You want to stretch the noodle out while you roll, being careful not to press down and flatten the dough rope. If you're finding the dough is too elastic and bouncing back in length, wrap it up and leave it to rest for 30 minutes. You'll find it much easier to roll after a short dough nap – don't we all function better after a little afternoon nap? Your first noodle might not be the best, but once you're on a roll …

Equipment: n/a

Level: easy

Make your desired quantity of semolina dough following the recipe on page 42.

- Cut off a small chunk of dough, approximately 5 cm x 2 cm, and roll it into a sausage, about 1.5 cm thick. Cut it in half or into thirds, depending on how long your dough sausage is. Keep the rest of the dough covered with a tea towel to stop it drying out.

- On a lightly floured work surface, roll the dough lengths, one by one, between the surface and the palms of your hands, gently pulling the dough outwards as you roll into approximately 15 cm-long noodles, about 3 mm thick. Your noodles will look slightly squiggly and uneven. Embrace it. Leave the noodles on a shallow tray well dusted with semolina flour to stop them sticking together. Cover with a tea towel to stop them drying out.

Busiate

Busiate belongs to the fusilli family, the coiled telephone cord pasta shapes. It hails from Sicily and is considered to be the oldest Sicilian homemade pasta. The name comes from 'busa', a type of reed that the pasta was originally wrapped around. Today, a wooden skewer does the trick. Sometimes if, for whatever reason, I don't get the pasta to roll around my skewer enough, I end up with a pasta that's a hybrid of busiate and maccheroni al ferretto – a hollow, thick handmade noodle. It doesn't really bother me, though, and I hope it doesn't bother you either. It is equally as impressive and still captures the sauce in its crevices.

Keep your skewer well floured and be careful not to put pressure on the dough when rolling as you don't want it sticking to your skewer.

Equipment: wooden skewer

Level: medium

Make your desired quantity of semolina dough following the recipe on page 42.

- Cut off a small piece of dough, approximately 5 cm x 2 cm, and roll it into a rope, about 5 mm thick. You may find it easier to cut the rope in half if it's getting too long. Keep the rest of the dough covered with a tea towel to stop it drying out.

- Cut the rope into 10–12 cm lengths.

- Place a length of dough in front of you at a 45-degree angle.

- Place the middle of a well-floured skewer horizontally on your dough, 1 cm away from the top. Using your finger, curl the top part of the dough rope over the skewer, then, using both hands, roll the skewer down towards you so the dough fully wraps around the skewer.

- Placing a little pressure on the skewer – not the dough – gently roll it back and forth with your hands to make the pasta longer and thinner.

- Carefully slide the pasta off of the skewer with your hand, while preserving the shape.

- Place the pasta on a floured work surface and repeat.

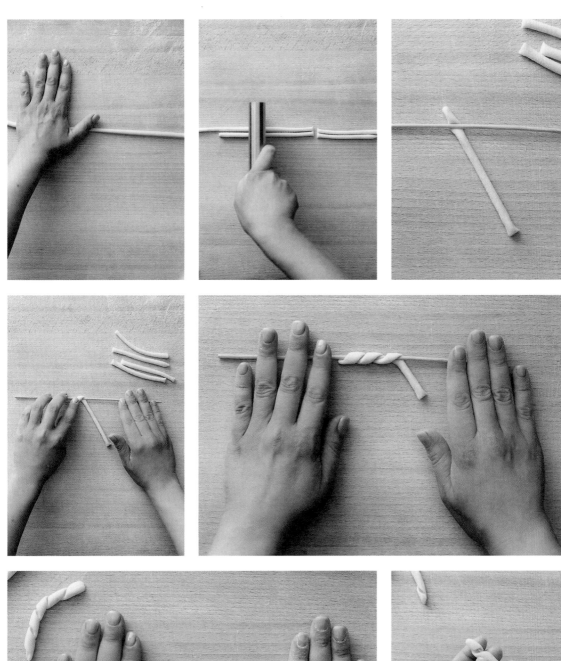
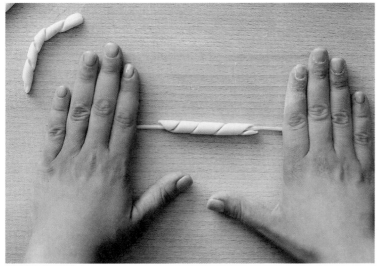

Cavatelli/Malloreddus

It's a fact that you will find the same pasta shapes all over Italy but with different names depending on where you are. Cavatelli literally means anything that is carved and hollowed out, and it can be made in a number of different ways – using fingers, knife or thumb. It comes from the south, namely Puglia, but in Sardinia the shape is called malloreddus. Technically, malloreddus have saffron in the dough, which turns the pasta a bright yellow. I rarely add saffron, which I guess means I should call it cavatelli but, hey, I first made it as malloreddus and I really love the story that accompanies it, so I always call the shape by this name. The tale goes that there was a tradition for brides to make a basket full of malloreddus to bring to the house of her new husband on their wedding night. They would then enjoy the pasta together from the same plate, a sign of the coming together of two families.

Cavatelli/malloreddus is a happy medium between gnocchi and pasta, with a lovely springy texture. It's deceptively easy to make, but looks impressive, which is why it is one of the hits I have on high rotation when I'm entertaining friends for Saturday Night Pasta.

You can use any number of things lying around the house to create a textured pattern on the pasta – sieves, zesters, a basket, chopsticks even – although I always reach for my trusty gnocchi board.

Equipment: gnocchi board

Level: easy–medium

Make your desired quantity of semolina dough following the recipe on page 42.

- Cut off a small chunk of dough, approximately 5 cm x 2 cm, and roll it into a rope about 1 cm thick. Keep the rest of the dough covered with a tea towel to stop it drying out.

- Cut the rope into 1 cm lengths.

- Lightly flour a gnocchi board and hold it up on an angle with the base resting on your work surface.

- Place a piece of dough at the top of the board. Place the side of your thumb on the dough, then drag the dough down the gnocchi board so it almost curls over your thumb, creating a ridged curl.

- Repeat, ensuring that your gnocchi board remains well floured.

73

Maccheroni a descita

This pasta shape is classed as another interpretation of cavatelli, as the pasta is also hollowed out. Likewise, it comes from Puglia and is also rolled into a rope before being cut and dragged across a surface using your fingers, leaving little finger imprints to catch your sauce. It's another charming example of the talents of Italian peasants and their cleverness for creating new shapes. In my research, I've also seen it called strascinati and raschiatelli, but considering I struggle to pronounce either I'm going to stick with maccheroni a descita. Sfoglina Julia, my pasta teacher, told me that you can make this pasta in a number of lengths, just using fewer or more fingers when pressing down. I also like that this pasta shape is unique to your fingerprint. I roll my rope to just under 1 cm thick and then cut the lengths to two fingers wide as it can get quite spongy if kept too big.

Equipment: n/a

Level: easy

Make your desired quantity of semolina dough following the recipe on page 42.

- Cut off a small chunk of dough, approximately 5 cm x 2 cm, and roll it into a rope, about 1 cm thick. Keep the rest of the dough covered with a tea towel to stop it drying out.

- Cut the rope into roughly 3 cm lengths, or use the width of two fingers as a guide and cut accordingly.

- Using your index and middle fingers, press into your dough, then drag it towards you to allow the dough to wrap around and hollow out. If your dough pieces are longer, you can use all three fingers – index, middle and ring.

- Do as the nonne do and flick away the pasta.

- Repeat. After you've got the hang of it, feel free to use both hands to double your speed.

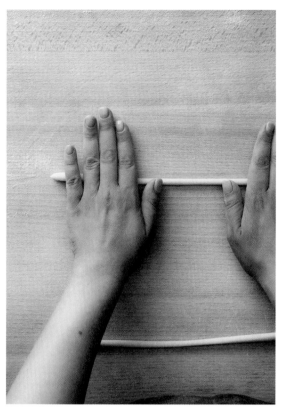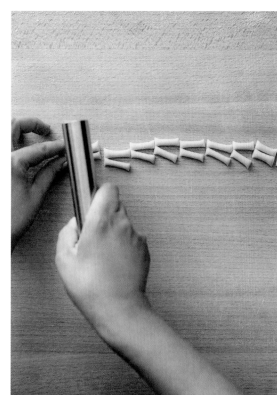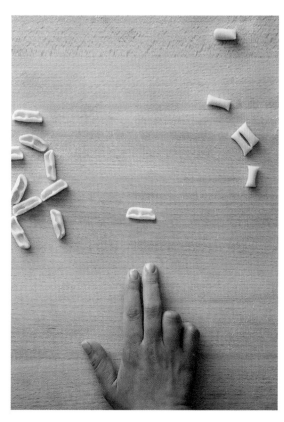

Orecchiette

Another pasta hailing from Puglia, orecchiette means 'little ears', with the shape resembling ear lobes. The pasta does an excellent job at cupping sauce, and you'll most often see it served with cime di rapa or broccoli. At pasta school, we made orecchiette with grano arso, a burnt wheat flour. Traditionally, peasants would go and collect what was left of the wheat after it had been burnt. They would then grind it up, creating a burnt flour that imparted a smoky note to the pasta. It's not an easy flour to source – I've yet to find it in Australia – so I always stick with semolina.

Orecchiette does take some practice. The first time I attempted it I had a full-blown tantrum at home by myself and literally threw a piece of the dough across the kitchen, but don't let this put you off.

All good things come to those who wait, meaning persistence and patience are key here. If I had taken a breath and kept going, I'm sure I would have got the hang of it that night. The next time I attempted it (at pasta school in Italy, when I was calm and relaxed), I picked it up easily. I then spent a good chunk of time practising my technique and now it is second nature. I encourage you to give this a go, but maybe first in the calmness of a solo Saturday Night Pasta.

Equipment: serrated table knife or butter knife

Level: medium

Make your desired quantity of semolina dough following the recipe on page 42.

- Cut off a small piece of dough, approximately 5 cm x 2 cm, and roll it into a rope, about 1.5 cm thick (much like the thickness of a pen). Keep the rest of the dough covered with a tea towel to stop it drying out.

- Cut the rope into 1.5 cm lengths.

- Place a piece of dough in a diamond shape in front of you. Using a serrated table or butter knife, place the serrated edge at the top of the dough, then place your index finger on top. Drag the knife down, allowing the pasta to start to curve around the knife. Stop when you are almost at the end of the pasta.

- Hold the knife and pasta up, then place your opposite thumb in the centre of the pasta and use your index and ring finger to invert the orecchiette to create a little cup. Flip onto a well-floured surface.

- Repeat; you'll get it after a few gos. The first one is never good, just like the first pancake.

Strozzapreti

There are so many wonderful legends about strozzapreti. With a name literally translating to 'priest strangler', you can't help but wonder how this pasta came about. Some say that after a long, hot day working in the fields, the women would sometimes come home to find a priest waiting to be fed, which was considered partial payment for land rents. This apparently angered the women so much that they would picture strangling the priests as they stuffed their faces (the shape is meant to resemble a wrung neck or a wrung-out towel that was then used to strangle someone). Another story goes that a priest found himself so hungry one day after wandering back and forth through the village that he ate the pasta with such voracity that he choked. Apparently, his servant then shifted into gear and struck him in the throat with her fist until he spat it out. Whichever tale you prefer, the name seems to reflect widespread opposition to the power that priests held during these times.

Strozzapreti can be made in a variety of ways using different flours and doughs – some regions even use bread or potatoes (if you google strozzapreti you'll see what I mean) – but this is how I make it. I find it the simplest and most satisfying method, especially when it's been a long week. Just like punching a boxing bag, the 'strangling' or rubbing of hands together in a swift movement does wonders for the soul.

Equipment: rolling pin, ruler

Level: medium

Make your desired quantity of semolina dough following the recipe on page 42.

- This is the only semolina dough shape that actually requires rolling. Much like an egg dough, you want to roll out your dough using a rolling pin until it is about 2 mm thick. I prefer to roll out the dough in batches to stop it drying out while I make my strozzapreti. In which case, cut your dough into thirds.

- Cut the rolled dough into 1 cm-wide strips. Leave the strips to 'cure' for 5 minutes.

- Hold up a strip of dough and pinch the top. Using an index finger and thumb, place the pinched top on the palm of your other hand. In one swift movement, run your hand forward over the pasta all the way to your pinky, which will roll or 'strangle' the pasta strip. Pinch the rolled pasta off (it should be roughly 6–7 cm long) and repeat the action with the remaining length of pasta hanging in your hands.

  One strip of pasta should make around four or five lengths of strozzapreti.

- Repeat.

Fregola

Fregola is the tiny, crumb-like pasta from Sardinia that's almost identical in appearance to pearl couscous, but cooked and served differently (couscous is steamed, whereas fregola is boiled and served in broth). It's made very differently to the other pastas in this book, as you sprinkle the flour with water and then rub it with your fingers to form small balls, no bigger than peppercorns. It is then toasted in the oven or left out in the sun to impart a nice nuttiness. It does require some patience and intuition, but don't confuse this with being complicated; it just means that it requires concentration and mindfulness. I find the process very cathartic, hence its place in SNP. To be honest, my balls vary in size and shape (let's call them irregular balls) so I just sift the finer crumbs out. Don't beat yourself up about it. There is an old Sardinian proverb that says, 'give me a husband, because I know how to make fregola'. For the record, I was already married when I learned how to make fregola.

Equipment: wide shallow bowl, sieve

Level: medium

You will need 125 g (1 cup) of semolina flour and 125 ml (½ cup) of water to make enough fregola for two people. You might not need all of the water.

- Preheat the oven to 150°C.

- Place your semolina flour in a wide shallow bowl, 30–40 cm wide (a wooden bowl is preferable as it creates good traction, but I'm going to assume most of you don't have a large shallow wooden bowl handy).

- Using one hand, sprinkle over about 1 tablespoon of water. With your other hand, use the tips of your fingers to drag the water through the semolina in a circular motion to create small irregular-shaped balls. Add a little more water while you keep dragging your fingers through, but don't get impatient and dump the water in all at once or you'll just create a big clump of dough. The trick is to work the water into the flour very slowly to allow small pieces of flour to clump together. Continue to add water, 1 tablespoon at a time, while dragging and stirring with your fingers.

- Continue this action until your flour is transformed into small peppercorn-ish-sized fregola. This can take upwards of 15 minutes, and if you are anything like me, you will end up with a range of sizes and shapes. Embrace it. Just don't have anything bigger than 1 cm in diameter.

- Place the fregola in a single layer on a baking tray and toast in the oven for 15–20 minutes, until it feels dry to the touch. I sift my fregola through a sieve to separate any of the tiny grains that didn't quite make it to fregola size. If you're feeling thrifty, these tiny grains can then be used to thicken soups.

Pasta Basics

A good understanding of the basics will enable you to stretch your pasta knowledge and give you the confidence to take your pasta game to the next level. These fundamentals have enhanced my understanding of how to make and cook pasta, and will help you navigate your way through your own pasta-making journey.

Shape vs sauce

Choosing the right pasta shape to match your sauce is a contentious issue. As many Italians will tell you, this makes the difference between an ordinary pasta dish and an extraordinary pasta dish. And while I do agree with this, I don't think it's as simple as one shape fits one sauce. Throughout Italy, from region to region and town to town, a pasta shape, although maybe with another name, will be paired with a different sauce. The combinations preferred by Italians are endless and everyone has their favourites.

As a result, there are an infinite number of interpretations and there are inevitably some pasta shapes that work well with a variety of sauces (I like to call these my workhorse pastas and I suggest many in this book). Having said that, there are some general guidelines to follow that will enhance your eating experience. These are based on how heavy the pasta is compared to the sauce and making sure that they are balanced. The principles state that thinner, more delicate pasta shapes and filled pastas (as you've already got flavour going on in the filling) are best suited to lighter and simpler sauces, such as oil- or butter-based sauces, broths or a light tomato sauce. Bigger, thicker pasta shapes with more texture can stand up to chunkier, richer sauces, such as a ragù. A thin spaghetti is a match made in heaven for vongole speckled with garlic and chilli, whereas orecchiette perfectly cups tiny florets of broccoli. Thick, long pastas, such as bucatini or pici, work well with richer sauces that have a kick, while curly strands, such as fusilli or busiate, catch chunky-style sauces in their curves and crevices. Then there are some shapes and sauces that are so deeply rooted in tradition that they are respected all over Italy. Tagliatelle al ragù is one of these, and you'd be hard pressed to find Emilia-Romagna's famed meat sauce served with anything other than tagliatelle.

Chefs tend to be much stricter and more uncompromising on the topic, but luckily for you and me (assuming you are also a home cook) we aren't bound by such sentiments. You could write a doorstop tome on pasta shapes and sauces – and indeed people have – but here is where I'm going to leave this subject. Similar to wine pairing, there is a point when it comes down to personal preference. This is especially true for spaghetti bolognese, arguably one of Australia's national dishes. And while I agree that spaghetti does nothing to enhance the richness and chunkiness of a good bol', at the end of the day we just really like it.

84

Dried vs fresh

This book was born from the meditative practice of making pasta by hand; however, I certainly don't discriminate between dried and fresh. I want to be realistic and inclusive, which is why I've included both options in my recipes, but I do want to address the dried vs fresh debate here first. You should not judge fresh as better than dried; they are merely different, and just like choosing a pasta shape, sometimes one or the other is better suited to a sauce. For me, dried pasta is the better choice for spaghetti vongole, as the finished texture gives a stronger bite against the oily sauce. Fresh pasta absorbs sauce more readily, so it's more suited to wet dishes, such as ragù or a tomato-based sauce.

Italians have always been experts at creating pasta shapes at home, but for those who are not an Italian nonna or skilled in finger acrobatics, dried pasta can give us many different shapes that we humble cooks wouldn't be able to achieve at home. Plus, I'm pretty sure when dried pasta came onto the shelves, Italian housewives were thrilled with their newfound freedom and time-saving packets of pasta.

When it comes to dried pasta, I always keep both a long, thin pasta and a chunkier, shorter one in the pantry at all times so I can ensure my shape enhances my sauce. My favourites include angel hair (or Capelli d'Angelo), which is the thinnest long pasta on the supermarket shelves (and a good replacement for fresh tagliolini), spaghetti, bucatini (a thicker, tube-like spaghetti) and linguine (for anything thicker than linguine I prefer to make it fresh). For shorter pasta, I love rigatoni, penne, fusilli and conchiglie (shells). Small pasta such as ditalini, risoni or fregola are also great to have on hand, especially when you've had a bad day (see my recipe on page 171). For my dried pasta suggestions in the recipes, I've chosen ones that are readily available; however, there is a whole universe of dried shapes that I encourage you to explore.

One thing to note is that you'll sometimes see 'peasant shapes' – those irregular pastas that are all made by hand, such as orecchiette and trofie – on some Italian delicatessen shelves. I recommend avoiding these, as they don't seem to cook very well – the outside gets too soft while the inside stays hard. Another point worth keeping in mind when you are making your sauce is that dried pasta absorbs less than fresh. Because of this, it means that dried pasta might require less oil, butter or pasta cooking water when tossing through your sauce.

Having said all this, I am obviously recommending that you give fresh pasta a go – the benefits were enough for me to write a book about it – but have you ever listened carefully to the sound of dried pasta being poured into a saucepan of boiling water after a long day? The Italians describe it as resembling a 'schiaffo' or slap with an open hand and I find it very satisfying indeed.

Dried pasta quantities

It can be hard to give precise quantities for dried pasta as it will vary between long and short pasta shapes. Typically, you want to weigh out 80 g dried pasta per person (so 160 g for two and 320 g for four people). This, of course, also depends on the quality of the pasta and how hungry you and your guests are, so let your appetite guide you here.

Cooking pasta

Here is my guide to cooking pasta. No doubt you have all cooked pasta before – throw it in boiling water, right? Well, yes, in theory, but there are some additional elements to think about to ensure you get the best out of the pasta you've just spent time making. These elements will lift your dish to restaurant-worthy pasta every time.

The saucepan
Take a large deep saucepan, fill it with water and set it over high heat. It's important that you use a large pan, so the pasta has plenty of room to move around, otherwise you risk it becoming claggy. If you don't have a large pan, cook your pasta in batches.

Bring the water to a lively boil. The pandemonium of the boiling water keeps the pasta moving and prevents it from sticking, which is important as the pasta releases starch while it cooks. They say to never watch a pan of boiling water, but watching those last stages when the water finally reaches boiling point is mesmerising. My sleep app has a 'boiling pot of water' sound, which I sometimes fall asleep to.

Salting
When the water is boiling, season it generously with salt. I can't prescribe precise amounts of salt for cooking pasta for a number of reasons: I don't know the size of your pan or how much water you are using, or how salty your salt is (it differs), so what I generally advise is to do as the Italians do and make it as salty as the sea. I know it seems like a lot, but remember that not all of this salt gets absorbed by the pasta as most of it goes down the drain, and seasoning your pasta is an important step. Pasta will taste dull and lifeless if cooked in under-salted water. However, one thing to note is to use slightly less salt if you are serving with a salty sauce – hello anchovies! I prefer to salt my water after it has come to the boil (otherwise it seems to take twice as long to boil), but it doesn't really make a difference. Always wait until the water returns to a lively boil before adding the pasta. You should never add oil to the water – it's a waste. Your pasta won't stick together if it's got enough room to move.

Cooking times

Fresh pasta only takes minutes to cook and there is not much leeway here. When it's ready, it's ready. You'll need to be present and focused; it only takes a minute or two and you could compromise all your hard work. Timing will all depend on your pasta shape, size and thickness. As a rough guide, allow 2 minutes for a thin egg pasta and roughly 4 minutes for filled egg pasta. Semolina pasta can also take about 4 minutes, but be wary as it will have more bite than fresh egg pasta. Dried pasta cooking times will be driven by your packet. I tend to cook dried pasta at least 2 minutes less than the recommended cooking time, but, really, I find the best way to test it is to fish out a strand and give it a nibble.

Al dente

Overcooking pasta isn't classed as a crime, but I sure as hell treat it as one. Pasta should always be cooked until al dente, which means to the tooth, or firm to the bite, unless stated otherwise. And if your recipe requires your pasta to bubble away in the sauce, then you should take it out when it's molto al dente, which means very al dente, almost slightly undercooked.

The firmness of dried pasta when cooked is very different to that of fresh pasta. Fresh pasta will never be as firm and chewy as dried so you should not compare the two. This is why a dried spaghetti pairs particularly well with an oil-based sauce and a fresh egg pasta is the perfect match for a wet ragù.

Pasta cooking water

Once cooked, you'll need to drain the pasta immediately. Alternatively, if I'm only cooking for myself or a few people then I like to use my tongs to grab the pasta, dripping with water, and fling it rather dramatically into my sauce for the final moments of cooking. Pasta cooking water is liquid gold. Pasta releases starch as it boils away, and when this starchy water meets your sauce it emulsifies everything and makes your dish the luxurious and silky pasta of your dreams. If you're cooking for a crowd, then it might be too overwhelming to grab it from the pan. Here, a colander comes in handy, but always, I repeat *always*, scoop out a cup of that liquid gold to have on hand to add to your sauce. Keep more than you think you'll need. It's hard for me to give exact quantities of water as it depends on the pasta (dried or fresh), the heat and how much fat you've added. But remember that you want your sauce to be loose and relaxed – just like you – and bear in mind that it will continue thickening as you put it on the table, especially with the addition of cheese.

Finishing your pasta

Having the sauce ready when your pasta is done is another vital step. As the great Marcella Hazan once said, 'there should be no pauses in the sequence of draining, saucing, serving and eating'. Pasta waits for no one. Cooked pasta should not be allowed to sit, or it will turn into a clump. You should never serve sauce on top of pasta so toss, toss, toss. Tossing your pasta through your sauce allows it to become one. Then add a little more pasta cooking water – you'll always be surprised at how much the pasta and sauce drink up. Toss some more, then stir in your cheese little by little and, if using, your butter or oil. Oh, and dress your pasta in sauce don't drown it. The pasta should be the star, not the sauce.

Serving pasta

Usually it will be just me and my bowl of pasta for dinner and I don't bother with anything else. However, if I have friends coming around for Saturday Night Pasta, I always serve crusty bread on the side to mop up the sauce. There's a name for this too: la scarpetta.

Salad should always be served after the pasta.

Damage control

Like yoga and Pilates, making pasta is about following a set of instructions and trusting your instincts about what feels good. This might mean making small adjustments and getting to know the dough (just like you know what works and feels right for your body). Despite measuring out your ingredients, there are a lot of things outside your control that can have an impact on the dough. The key here is not to panic; do not have a meltdown or lose the plot, okay? So, relax, pour a glass of wine or make a cup of tea and know that there are always ways to realign. The tip here is to take note and learn what could have affected the end result of your dough. This will help you improve. Much like any exercise, practice makes perfect.

My eggs spilled out of the flour well

Ahh, your flour well has collapsed and you have egg pouring out over your work surface and onto the floor. Try and rescue as much as you can and throw it back on the dough. You'll need to estimate how much egg you lost – was it the whole egg or do you think you could replace it with some water? This is the moment you'll need to use your senses. Continue to combine the remaining egg and flour. If things are feeling extra dry, add a tablespoon of water at a time until it comes back to a neutral dough. If this is the sort of thing you think could happen to you, combine your egg and flour in a large bowl first.

My dough is too dry/hard

The air flow might have dried things out, or perhaps your eggs weren't big enough (did you weigh them?). Either way, do not panic. A simple mist of water or wetting your hands before continuing to knead should solve the problem. Remember, don't flood the dough – add water little by little to give it a chance. The dough will continue to hydrate during the resting time, too.

My dough is too wet/sticky

Humidity could have played a part here or maybe your eggs had too much liquid in their whites. A sprinkle of flour and further kneading will help the dough. Again, start small as you don't want to get into the game of more flour, more liquid, more flour, more liquid.

My pasta is sticking to the surface

Your dough most likely has too much moisture – see the above point. Regarding surfaces, I prefer to work with wood as I find other surfaces retain moisture that can make the pasta stick. Dust your surface with flour. I actually prefer to dust with semolina flour even when I'm making an egg dough as I find it doesn't absorb as much into the pasta. Use a pastry scraper to move the pasta – it does less damage than your hands.

My semolina dough is hard to roll out/keeps bouncing back

Having trouble rolling out a rope of semolina dough? You may have worked it too much, in which case it needs a longer rest. Simply wrap it up in plastic wrap and leave to rest for another 20–30 minutes before trying again.

My dough is cracking at the sides as I roll it through the machine

It's drying out, so you will need to work quickly and ensure that any sheets you have finished rolling are covered to slow this process down. It's not a big drama, you can easily trim the sides off, but take this as a lesson.

My tagliolini or tagliatelle rollers aren't cutting very well when I run the dough through the machine

Your dough is too soft, so you will need to let it cure for about 5–10 minutes, depending on the weather. This should help them cut better.

My paccheri or garganelli are collapsing

I sometimes find that the dough can be a little too wet or soft to hold the hollow shapes of paccheri or garganelli. To keep my hollows, I roll the dough a little thicker than what is 'recommended' by the professionals and I leave it to cure slightly to build up some strength. You don't want to leave it to dry so much that the edges crack – 5–8 minutes, depending on the weather, should be fine. You will notice the difference, but you might need to swipe the seal with a wet finger to encourage the dough to stick.

My dough sheets are cracking

Ahh, you let them dry out too much. There's not much saving here except to cut them up, maltagliati style (see page 59), and throw them in the boiling water.

My filled pasta broke open when cooking

You've either let some air into the filling or it wasn't sealed properly. When making your filled pasta, take care to squeeze out all the air and push down to give it a good seal. A brush of water along the edge helps hydrate the pasta and make it sticky.

I've made too much pasta

Okay, you've made too much. Pasta dough can be frozen. Simply wrap it tightly in plastic wrap and store it in a zip-lock bag in the freezer. For uncooked pasta, it's best to lay it out on a tray to dry. If you've made egg pasta you can also freeze it spread out on a tray. Once frozen, put it in a zip-lock bag and keep it in the freezer for a midweek meal. Italians don't like waste, so even left-over cuttings of egg pasta are turned into maltagliati, a pasta shape meaning 'badly cut' (see page 59). These offcuts can be dried and saved for meals like soups or even other pasta dishes.

I'm not a big fan of reheating cooked pasta, so I prefer to throw it in a pasta bake (see page 196) or a frittata.

My sauce tastes unbalanced

As in life, balance is important in pasta sauces. Sometimes tomatoes, both canned and fresh, can be very acidic. To balance them out, a pinch of sugar does the trick. Something feeling a little flat? A spritely squeeze of lemon juice can bring out attitude in a dish.

Ingredients and Equipment

Here is a list of my go-to ingredients and recommended equipment to help get you started on your Saturday Night Pasta journey.

Ingredients

Canned tomatoes

I prefer to use whole peeled Italian tomatoes. You'll notice throughout this book that my tomato of choice is cherry, so I am always delighted when I find a can of cherry tomatoes or baby romas. I don't like using diced tomatoes, as they are normally made with the scraps and, as a result, just aren't as good.

Cheese

Parmigiano Reggiano is the king of cheese in Italy. It's the one I always have on hand and I pretty much finish all my pasta dishes with it (with the exception of seafood; I agree with the Italians on that point). Parmigiano Reggiano has a sharp, nutty taste and savoury umami flavour that I just love, and I could quite happily nibble away at a wedge. I'll even feature it as a dessert alongside poached pears.

Grana Padano is another Italian cheese that you'll find on the cheese shelf. It's usually a bit cheaper, milder and less crumbly than Parmigiano Reggiano, but it still makes a good option. **Pecorino Romano** is a sheep's milk cheese used in central and southern Italy. Technically, it should be used to finish off hardy pasta dishes from these regions, such as guanciale, tomato and chilli (Amatriciana) and carbonara.

All of these cheeses are aged to develop flavour and texture. Take note of the differences between a young, spritely pecorino, a richer Grana Padano, which can be aged between 8 and 20 months, and an intense Parmigiano Reggiano, which is aged between 12 and 36 months, resulting in a super-rich cheese that has achieved its fullest flavour potential.

Finally, there is the cheese simply labelled '**parmesan**', which you can find on all supermarket shelves. As I'm investing myself in the pasta I'm cooking, I prefer to use the real Italian stuff. You can really taste the difference.

Always grate cheese fresh. Like fat-free dairy, there is no place in this world for pre-grated cheese.

I won't always give exact measurements. This is because, a) I find it incredibly annoying and unnecessary to measure out freshly grated cheese and b) I want you to use your own intuition when finishing off your pasta dish, especially as the amount of cheese can be a personal preference. But for the sake of consistency, a good handful is about 80 g or a loosely packed cup.

Eggs

Always fresh and free range, preferably organic. I can't stress enough the importance of using good-quality eggs, particularly as egg pasta only features two ingredients. If a chicken has enjoyed a varied diet pecking at a good array of vegetables, you'll end up with intensely coloured yolks that are rich in nutrients and healthy fats. I once came across egg yolks that were almost red and, as a result, I ended up with the brightest, sunniest dough. When I asked what the chickens ate, the farmer told me he fed them carrots and red capsicums! I always beg, borrow and steal eggs from friends who have chickens. The results are incomparable. I've recently discovered that the heat of summer can also affect the colour of egg yolks, so you may find that your egg yolks are richer and brighter in winter.

Fat – butter and olive oil

Have you ever questioned the difference between a pasta you've enjoyed at a restaurant and the pasta you make at home? The difference mostly lies in the last few steps of cooking. The secret to a silky, glossy sauce is the emulsification of fat, pasta cooking water and cheese. I didn't realise butter was a key ingredient in pasta until I watched the chefs at OTTO in Sydney add a generous knob at the end of cooking, which resulted in something rich and shiny. Butter is normally used to finish pasta dishes in northern Italy, whereas a good-quality extra-virgin olive oil rounds off dishes in the south.

I always use extra-virgin olive oil in my cooking. It comes in a range of flavour profiles – mild, peppery, grassy – and what you choose really comes down to personal preference. I prefer a mild and mellow extra-virgin olive oil that has fewer bitter notes, as this complements my pasta rather than overpowering it. I use a quality but affordable oil to cook with and then save my really good-quality stuff to finish off delicate pasta dishes. When buying extra-virgin olive oil, always look for dark bottles as the oil doesn't like light. Know where your oil comes from and look at the harvest date (extra-virgin olive oil is not like wine – it doesn't age well). Finally, make sure it is truly extra-virgin olive oil, as a lot of supermarket brands will market their oils as 'light', 'pure' or as just regular 'olive oil'. Avoid these impostors.

Flour

I mainly use two types of flour when making pasta. For egg pasta dough I use Tipo 00, which is a finely milled, extra-soft wheat flour that you can find at Italian delicatessens. For semolina pasta I use semolina or semola di grano duro, which is a harder, coarser durum wheat flour. It is more yellow in colour and structured differently to Tipo 00, and therefore does not develop gluten as easily. You'll notice the difference straight away. Find it in Italian delicatessens or buy online.

Pangrattato or breadcrumbs

Italian peasants historically used pangrattato (a topping of breadcrumbs) as an economical alternative to Parmigiano Reggiano because the cheese was simply too expensive. I use both for added texture and flavour. When I say breadcrumbs, I'm not talking about the sawdust-type dried breadcrumbs that you buy in a packet. I'm talking about breadcrumbs made from real loaves of bread. I always keep a bag of breadcrumbs in the freezer and I encourage you to do the same. It has become a weekly habit to pulse up my left-over bread into crumbs and throw them in a zip-lock bag. The whole exercise takes 5 minutes and it means they are always on hand to transform any dish – and I'm not just talking about pasta. There is no need to defrost your breadcrumbs, simply tip them directly into your hot oil. When toasting breadcrumbs, I'll often flavour them with ingredients I have to hand: anchovy fillets, chilli and garlic, for example, all make the most excellent additions.

Salt

I use Kosher salt to salt my cooking water and when I'm adding salt to a sauce. Sea salt flakes are used to finish off dishes, as they give a lovely crunch. I was told that Kosher salt is the purest salt available as it has no additives, unlike table salt which commonly contains anticaking agents to prevent clumps.

Equipment

Digital scales

Electronic scales take the guess work out of measurements and minimise room for error. I'm not as good as the Italian nonne who can simply use their hands to measure out ingredients.

Dutch oven

I can't live without my cast-iron pan; it is my most-used piece of kitchen equipment. The advantage of cooking with cast iron is the beautiful even heat it gives, meaning less chance of scorching those sauces. Cooking pasta sauces in it is a real pleasure, as it stops me flinging sauce everywhere when I toss the pasta through. It's also a cinch to clean – well, for Tom to clean.

Gnocchi board

This is a small ridged wooden board needed to make cavatelli/malloreddus, garganelli and other semolina pasta shapes and, of course, gnocchi. The ridges create grooves in the pasta, which the sauce adheres to.

Pasta board

Pasta boards are about 80 cm wide, with a lip that hangs over the edge of your kitchen bench so the board doesn't slip around when you are kneading and rolling out your dough. The idea is that the board should only ever be used to roll pasta, therefore keeping it free of contamination from other ingredients. Of course, a pasta board is not a requirement, but it does making rolling out pasta enjoyable. I prefer to make pasta on a clean wooden bench. Never use a plastic chopping board.

Pasta dowel

This instrument is for wrapping your dough around to make garganelli or paccheri, although I find that a wooden spoon handle also does the trick.

Pasta machine

It's worthwhile investing in a pasta machine, as it requires virtually no skill to produce beautiful egg pasta on your very first go. You don't need to spend hundreds of dollars either; there are some great affordable machines on the market for less than $100. I promise this won't become another kitchen gadget that will gather dust in the back of your cupboard. If you love pasta, it will fast become a kitchen favourite – mine takes pride of place on my bookshelf. Never wash your pasta machine, a quick dusting and wipe will ensure it lasts for years.

Pasta saucepan

Use a large saucepan or stockpot – preferably 5–7 litre capacity – to allow the pasta to move around freely.

Pastry cutter

Also known as a bench scraper, a pastry cutter is useful for cutting and moving the dough and finished pasta around. It also makes you feel very professional.

Rolling pin

A long rolling pin without handles is great for rolling out dough, and it's especially important if you don't own a pasta machine.

Square metal skewer

This is helpful for making busiate, although a well-floured wooden skewer also works well.

SATURDAY NIGHT PASTA RECIPES

These are some of my favourite sauces I make for Saturday Night Pasta. My mood very much influences what I cook. When I'm feeling spritely and energetic, I find I want something that cooks in the same time as my pasta. When I need something uplifting, I go for a dish that is fresh and bright. If I'm needing some restoration, then I will most likely head for a ragù. For total distraction, it needs to be something that absorbs me in the process. And when I need comfort, it has to be a recipe that requires very little. None of it is meant to be challenging, which means it shouldn't overwhelm you or stress you out. As I cook with my mood, serving sizes change throughout the recipes, but as cooking pasta sauces is relaxed in nature, it's no problem to increase the quantities.

Following on from that point, I'd encourage you to use these recipes as templates and not as strict guides. Things don't need to be obsessively exact. Cook with intuition and ease. This is the sort of cooking you could do a little bit tipsy or when friends are around to distract you. These sauces are forgiving. If you want to add some chilli, go ahead, I always do. No rosemary? No worries, what about thyme? Do the clams look better than the mussels? Use them instead. Most of the time, it's going to be the ingredient that tells you what's best. There's no use reaching for out-of-season tomatoes. They'll be watery and dull, and you'll be unhappy.

In the following recipes, I've recommended my favourite pasta shapes for the sauce to be served with – both fresh and dried. Traditionalists might disagree, but it's what I like, and Saturday Night Pasta does not come with a set of rules. You might find you prefer a different combination, and that's just fine by me.

Cavolo nero, garlic, egg yolk

In this carb-conscious world, somewhere between zoodles and cauliflower rice, eating pasta became a rebellious act. Thankfully, these dark days seem to be passing, with more people taking comfort in pasta (and I'm assuming that by reading this book, you are too). Maybe it's the familiarity or pasta's approachability and versatility. Or are people just enjoying a bowl of pasta for what it is – delicious?

This brilliantly green pasta sauce is brought together with an egg yolk, and it feeds you in a way that 'clean eating' never will. Just like a carbonara, the egg will cook from the residual heat as you toss it through the hot pasta. The result is a rich and vibrant sauce that coats each strand. It's important that your eggs are fresh, free range and preferably organic. If you are uncomfortable eating raw egg, some dollops of ricotta or mascarpone are a good alternative. A few nuggets of creamy feta would also be a nice addition if that's what you have in the fridge.

Serves 2

2 garlic cloves
1 bunch of cavolo nero,
    leaves stripped
2 egg yolks
1 tablespoon extra-virgin olive oil
zest of 1 lemon
handful of grated Parmigiano
    Reggiano, plus extra to serve
sea salt and freshly ground
    black pepper
pinch of chilli flakes (optional)

FRESH PASTA FOR 2
tagliolini, tagliatelle, linguine

DRIED PASTA FOR 2
angel hair, linguine, spaghetti

Bring a large saucepan of water to a lively boil and season as salty as the sea.

Peel the garlic by smashing the cloves with the flat part of a knife – they should almost pop out of their skins. Throw the peeled garlic cloves and cavolo nero leaves into the boiling water and watch the hard, dark leaves turn a vibrant green and flop with the rise and fall of the bubbles. Cook for 5 minutes, then, using tongs, grab the dripping wet leaves and garlic and throw them into a blender.

Keep that now-green pan of water boiling, ready for your pasta.

Now is a good time to crack your eggs and separate the yolks. I prefer to separate eggs using my hands, as I find I can be more delicate than flipping them between the two shell halves. Keep the egg whites for another day.

Back to the sauce. Add the olive oil and lemon zest to the blender and blitz the whole thing up for about 3 minutes, until creamy and smooth. Add the Parmigiano Reggiano, plus a pinch of salt and pepper and the chilli, if using. Give it one last blitz to combine, then taste to check your seasoning and add more salt if needed.

Meanwhile, add your pasta to the boiling water and cook until al dente.

As a safety net, scoop out 250 ml (1 cup) of the pasta cooking water, as you might need it to loosen up your sauce. Drain the pasta and throw it back in the pan, along with the green sauce. Give everything a good swirl, allowing the pasta to gulp up the sauce and adding the reserved cooking water if needed. You want it to be loose and relaxed, just like you. Give it another dusting of Parmigiano Reggiano before one final swirl.

Divide the pasta between bowls and carefully nestle the raw egg yolk on top of each pasta nest. Add a final dusting of Parmigiano Reggiano and serve immediately.

Burnt butter, tomato, hazelnuts

Butter is a wonderful thing. A knob to finish off any pasta sauce will give a silky, shiny result. But burnt butter is something else. It takes these cherry tomatoes to a wonderfully nutty and intense place. The hazelnuts top off this nutty ride, but you can leave them out if you prefer.

Serves 2

35 g hazelnuts
80 g salted butter
500 g cherry tomatoes, halved, smaller ones left whole
4 oregano sprigs, leaves picked
2 garlic cloves, finely chopped
sea salt
handful of grated Parmigiano Reggiano, plus extra to serve

FRESH PASTA FOR 2
strozzapreti, linguine, tagliatelle

DRIED PASTA FOR 2
fettuccine, linguine, spaghetti

Preheat the oven to 180°C fan-forced.

Spread the hazelnuts in a single layer on a baking tray. Roast for about 10 minutes or until the hazelnuts are lightly toasted and the skins have started to crack. Tip the hazelnuts onto a clean tea towel and use the tea towel to rub and remove the skins (I find the skins to be too bitter, but this step is, of course, optional). Roughly chop the hazelnuts and set aside.

Heat a large frying pan over medium–high heat, then add the butter and let it melt. Once it starts to spit and splatter, reduce the heat to medium–low and give the butter a gentle stir. After about 4–5 minutes, the butter will start to turn a deep brown and smell nutty.

Add the tomato and oregano and cook for 5 minutes. Once the tomato has started to release its juice, add the garlic and season with salt. Adding the garlic now stops it burning from the shock of the hot butter. Let it simmer and mingle together for about 10 minutes.

Meanwhile, bring a large saucepan of water to a lively boil and season as salty as the sea. Add the pasta and cook until al dente. Drain the pasta, reserving 125 ml (½ cup) of the cooking water.

Toss the pasta through the tomato mixture, along with the Parmigiano Reggiano and half the pasta cooking water to loosen the whole thing up, adding more water if needed. Give the mixture a strong stir to create a sauce that's glossy and impossibly creamy, clinging to each and every strand.

Serve topped with the roasted hazelnuts and a last-minute snowfall of Parmigiano Reggiano.

Asparagus, fried egg, brown butter, walnut

This is the Coco Chanel of pasta dishes – simple, yet perfectly at home in the most elegant of restaurants. Mademoiselle Gabrielle 'Coco' Chanel's famous piece of advice was that before leaving the house, you should look in the mirror and take one thing off. She believed that simplicity was the key to true elegance. The Italians have long adopted the same philosophy, not to fashion but to food, and it's an approach that I also try to extend to living. I realised that when you leave things behind and refocus on the ordinary everyday – the smell of a dewy spring morning, the sparkly stars at night, your morning coffee, the excitement of eating a dish you've been waiting for all day, or that feeling when you fall into boisterous, magnificent laughter with friends that you've known for years – it becomes clear how simple life can be and how few things are really in your control to worry about. Overcomplicating life, much like a pasta sauce, can only lead to an imbalance, and that's the total opposite of elegance.

This dish is best enjoyed in asparagus season, which means spring, thank you very much (don't be fooled by the expensive Peruvian or Mexican imported versions that sit on supermarket shelves year round). I prefer the thin, almost wild-looking asparagus that bends with the noodle. If you only have thick spears, you can shave them to achieve a similar result, but that is, of course, optional. For those who have not had the pleasure of tasting walnut oil, it's a revelation, giving a tender kiss of walnut to your dish without the occasional bitterness of the raw nut.

Serves 2

1 bunch of asparagus – choose
    thin spears over fat spears
    if you can
2 tablespoons salted butter
1 teaspoon extra-virgin olive oil
2 eggs
2 tablespoons walnut oil
handful of grated Parmigiano
    Reggiano, plus extra to serve
sea salt and freshly ground
    black pepper
2 walnuts, to serve (optional)

FRESH PASTA FOR 2
linguine, strozzapreti, tagliatelle

DRIED PASTA FOR 2
linguine, spaghetti

Bring a large saucepan of water to a lively boil and season as salty as the sea.

Snap the ends off the asparagus (they will naturally break where the stem goes from tender to woody). Discard the woody ends.

Add the asparagus to the boiling water and blanch for 1 minute until just tender – did you notice how I said blanch? Do not commit the heinous crime of overcooking your asparagus. The spears should be bright green, strong and crisp, not floppy and limp. Pluck out the asparagus and refresh under cold running water. Set aside.

Cook your pasta in the same boiling water until al dente.

Melt the butter in a frying pan, along with the olive oil to stop it burning, until it starts to brown. Add the eggs and fry, sunny-side up, for 2 minutes. The whites need to be cooked, but the yolks should be just set.

Reserve 250 ml (1 cup) of the pasta cooking water, then drain the pasta and return it to the saucepan, along with the asparagus, walnut oil and Parmigiano Reggiano. Season with salt and pepper, then add 125 ml (½ cup) of the cooking water and give everything a strong swirl. Add a little more cooking water if you feel it's needed.

Divide the pasta between bowls and top with the fried eggs, burnt butter from the pan and extra Parmigiano Reggiano. Finely grate over the walnuts, if using, and serve immediately. Pasta waits for no one.

Basic tomato sauce, stracciatella, pangrattato

There are so many ways to make a tomato sauce. You can use fresh tomatoes or canned, but should you use onion or garlic, or both? What about the sofrito? That base of carrot, celery and onion, the backbone of Italian cooking. And what herbs? Basil, thyme or parsley? And do you add them at the start or at the end? Some cooks blend the sauce for a velvety finish, others prefer a good chunky texture. Some finish their sauce with olive oil, others with a knob of butter. Then what about the cooking times? Fast and furious or slow and steady? The answers are really all up to you.

Here I give you my basic, no-fuss tomato sauce: canned tomatoes, garlic, basil and butter (I like the gloss butter gives) with a medium cooking time. Serve adorned with a generous dollop of stracciatella or buffalo mozzarella and a sprinkling of crisp, golden breadcrumbs.

Serves 4

3 garlic cloves
100 ml extra-virgin olive oil, plus extra for drizzling
400 g canned whole peeled tomatoes
2 tablespoons unsalted butter
1 basil sprig
sea salt
2 slices of day-old crusty bread, such as sourdough (I prefer fresh breadcrumbs, but panko breadcrumbs are a good substitute)
zest of 1 lemon
125 g stracciatella or buffalo mozzarella
grated Parmigiano Reggiano, to serve

FRESH PASTA FOR 4
reginette (mafaldine), busiate, tagliatelle

DRIED PASTA FOR 4
any long pasta

Heat a heavy-based saucepan over medium heat. Finely chop two of the garlic cloves.

When the pan is hot, add 2 tablespoons of the olive oil and the chopped garlic and sizzle for 20 seconds, then empty in the can of tomatoes to stop the garlic from burning. Fill the can halfway with water and pour that in, too. Give everything a big stir and take a deep breath. Add the butter, basil and a generous pinch of salt. Reduce the heat to low, cover with a lid and leave to simmer for 30 minutes while you get on with the rest of the recipe.

Bring a large saucepan of water to a lively boil and season as salty as the sea.

Meanwhile, cut the bread into chunks. Using a food processor, pulse the bread intro breadcrumbs ranging from very fine to slightly bigger.

Heat the remaining 3 tablespoons of olive oil in a large frying pan over medium–high heat. Throw in the remaining whole garlic clove, along with the breadcrumbs, and sauté for 5 minutes or until golden and crisp. Drain the breadcrumbs on a piece of paper towel and allow to cool. Discard the garlic clove.

When the sauce is ready, cook the pasta until al dente. Using tongs, fling the pasta directly into the sauce, along with 125 ml (½ cup) of the cooking water and the lemon zest. Toss the pasta in the sauce until it is really well coated and the sauce sticks to each strand.

Divide the pasta among bowls. Plop a heaped tablespoon of stracciatella or buffalo mozzarella in the centre of each bowl and top with the breadcrumbs. Grate Parmigiano Reggiano over the top and drizzle with extra-virgin olive oil.

Basil pesto and ricotta ravioli, lemon butter

I know that the thought of making ravioli can put some people in a bad place mentally – and I'm not going to sugar-coat it, making filled pasta takes more time and patience then the other dishes in this book. But more time does not necessarily mean more difficult. It means that you should take it slowly and not rush the process.

This triangle-shaped ravioli is easy to master. All you need to do is cut out squares of pasta, place a little filling in the middle, then fold each square into a triangle. There is no tricky assembling or finger acrobatics required here. Once you've mastered this technique, you can move on to a world of other filled pastas.

As I've suggested below, work in steps and leave yourself plenty of time. The filling can be made ahead of time (and of course substituted for something else – ricotta and spinach? crab and mascarpone? pumpkin? potato?). Whatever you choose, just keep your filling on the dry side and remember to not overfill your ravioli. When in season, ripped up zucchini flowers thrown in the lemon butter at the last minute are a wonderful addition.

I've also given a bonus recipe here – a very basic basil pesto. I always blitz up a batch whenever I've got an abundance of fresh basil. The recipe gives you enough for two pasta meals for two, as there was no point making the quantities smaller than they already are. And besides, pesto tossed through pasta makes the easiest of weeknight dinners.

Serves 2

120 g full-fat ricotta
sea salt and freshly ground
  black pepper
Tipo 00 flour, for dusting
70 g salted butter
1 lemon

Basic basil pesto

30 g pine nuts
35–40 g (1 cup) basil leaves
1 garlic clove, peeled
zest of 1 lemon
40 g (½ cup) grated Parmigiano
  Reggiano, plus extra to serve
3 tablespoons extra-virgin
  olive oil
sea salt

FRESH EGG PASTA DOUGH FOR 2

Make the egg pasta dough as described on page 34, leaving it to rest for 30 minutes while you make the filling.

To make the pesto, preheat the oven to 180°C fan-forced. Spread the pine nuts on a baking tray and roast for 5 minutes, keeping a careful eye on them. Remove from the oven and set aside for 5–10 minutes, until cool enough to handle.

Transfer the pine nuts to a food processor and add the basil, garlic, lemon zest and Parmigiano Reggiano and blitz until finely chopped and fragrant. This can also be done using a mortar and pestle. Empty the mixture into a bowl and pour in the olive oil while you stir everything together. Season to taste with salt, then set aside.

To make the ravioli filling, place the ricotta in a bowl, stir through 3 tablespoons of the basil pesto and season with salt and pepper. I like to transfer the filling to a piping bag or a zip-lock bag with a corner cut off to squeeze out the mixture, but a teaspoon works, too. The filling can be kept in the fridge until ready.

When making ravioli, it's important to keep your pasta dough from drying out, which happens quickly. To avoid this, I like to roll a sheet, make the ravioli, then roll the next sheet. Always ensure that the dough you are not using is wrapped up, so it won't dry out. Take your time with each step as this limits room for mistakes, and enjoy the process. Follow the instructions for rolling out the pasta on page 38, until your pasta is 1 mm thick.

Lay out your first pasta sheet on a lightly floured work surface. Using a pastry cutter or a knife and a ruler, cut out 7 cm squares of pasta.

Pipe or spoon a large olive-sized blob of filling into the middle of each square. If your dough is on the dry side, using a pastry brush or your finger, run a tiny dab of water around each blob of filling.

Position a pasta square as a diamond in front of you. Using your thumb and index finger, fold the bottom corner up over the filling to make a triangle. Seal the pasta by pressing down around the filling with your two index fingers. Take care to push all the air out – this is one of the most important steps to master when making filled pasta. If you like, you can neaten up the triangles with a swift run of a knife or a fluted pastry cutter. See overleaf for a visual guide.

Lay out your ravioli on a floured chopping board or a tea towel, making sure they're not touching, then repeat with the remaining pasta and filling. Do not put the ravioli in the fridge.

Bring a large saucepan of water to a lively boil and season as salty as the sea. Cook the ravioli for 4–5 minutes or until just al dente.

Meanwhile, melt the butter in a generous-sized frying pan over medium heat. When the butter starts to foam, zest in the lemon, then taste and season with salt and pepper.

Using a slotted spoon, transfer the pasta straight into the lemon butter, adding just a splash of the cooking water to bring it all together. Cut the zested lemon in half and squeeze in half the juice (about 1 tablespoon). Taste, and add more if you like.

Divide the ravioli between bowls. Shower with Parmigiano Reggiano, grind over some pepper and serve.

Note: The ravioli can be frozen. Simply lay out on a tray to freeze and, once frozen, seal in a zip-lock bag. They can then be cooked from frozen – just add an extra minute or two to the cooking time.

Fresh tomato, goat's curd, basil

The food we dream of when we think about Italy tends towards simplicity and makes use of the humblest ingredients: spaghetti tossed with olive oil, garlic and chilli, or ripe summer tomatoes and basil heaped on toasted country bread. Yet so often when we cook at home, we feel that it just can't be this simple; that it needs to have more steps, more ingredients, more technique, otherwise it's simply not worthy to serve to others. How wrong this is.

'Keep it simple, stupid' is a design principle referring to the idea that most systems work best without unnecessary complexities. For me, this saying extends well past design and into cooking and everyday life. However, when things are kept simple it means there is nowhere to hide. Only the best will do. So this recipe should only be made in the height of summer, when tomatoes are ripe, the basil is heady and the weather is warm. It should be eaten barefoot in the sun as a reminder that it's the simple things in life that matter.

More often than not, I make this just for myself, but it's easily adaptable to serve more. I prefer cherry tomatoes, as I find them sweeter, but use the best tomatoes you can find. A sprinkle of chilli flakes is a nice finish, too.

Serves 1

1 garlic clove
150 g cherry tomatoes or the best summer-ripe tomatoes you can find, chopped
¼ bunch of basil, leaves picked, plus extra leaves to serve
2 tablespoons extra-virgin olive oil, plus extra for drizzling
sea salt and freshly ground black pepper
1 tablespoon goat's curd
grated Parmigiano Reggiano, to serve
chilli flakes, for sprinkling (optional)

FRESH PASTA FOR 1
busiate, fettuccine, linguine, strozzapreti

DRIED PASTA FOR 1
fusilli, linguine, spaghetti

Cut the garlic clove in half and rub it around a large serving bowl, to impart the scent of garlic. Add the tomato to the bowl, along with the garlic, basil and olive oil. Generously season with salt. Let the mixture sit at room temperature for 30–60 minutes, to allow the flavours to meld.

Bring a large saucepan of water to a lively boil and season as salty as the sea. Add the pasta and cook until al dente.

Remove the garlic from the tomato mixture and discard. Add blobs of goat's cheese to the tomato mixture in anticipation of the hot pasta that will fall on top.

Using tongs, pluck the pasta out of the rapid bubbles and drop it directly onto the tomato mixture. Give everything a big toss, adding a scoop of cooking water if needed to loosen things up. Season with salt and pepper, then top with extra basil leaves, a drizzle of extra-virgin olive oil, a sprinkle of Parmigiano Reggiano and a few chilli flakes, if you like, and serve.

Zucchini, fried capers, mint

Someone should package up and sell fried capers. They are highly snackable – salty, briny and delicious. Here, they not only add a salty pop to the finished dish but also a lovely contrasting crunch against the soft zucchini. I like to cut my zucchini using the julienne cutter on a mandoline so I have long noodle-like strands, which mimic the pasta. Grating zucchini on a wider setting would work, too. This is my playful nod to the zucchini noodle craze.

Serves 2

3 tablespoons extra-virgin olive oil, plus extra for drizzling
80 g (½ cup) capers, rinsed, drained and patted dry
2 garlic cloves, finely chopped
1 bird's eye chilli, deseeded and finely chopped (use half if you prefer less heat)
2 zucchini, julienned
sea salt
¼ bunch of mint, leaves picked and finely chopped
zest and juice of 1 lemon
handful of grated Parmigiano Reggiano, plus extra to serve

FRESH PASTA FOR 2
strozzapreti, linguine, tagliolini

DRIED PASTA FOR 2
linguine, spaghetti

Heat 2 tablespoons of the olive oil in a large frying pan over medium–high heat. Add the capers and sauté for 8–10 minutes, until brown and crisp. Using a slotted spoon, scoop out the capers onto paper towel and leave to drain.

Bring a large saucepan of water to a lively boil and season as salty as the sea. Add the pasta and cook until al dente.

Meanwhile, add the remaining 1 tablespoon of olive oil to the frying pan, along with the garlic and chilli, and cook for 1 minute. Add the zucchini, season with salt and cook, tossing frequently, for 2–3 minutes.

Drain the pasta, reserving 125 ml (½ cup) of the cooking water. Toss the pasta in the zucchini mixture with a splash of the reserved cooking water, the mint, lemon zest, a squeeze of lemon juice and the Parmigiano Reggiano. Give everything a good stir, adding more cooking water if you need to loosen things up.

Serve the pasta with a drizzle of olive oil, the extra Parmigiano Reggiano and the fried capers scattered over the top.

Spiced tomato, panko breadcrumbs

When I was growing up, a bunch of us would meet regularly after school at a local pasta bar. The thought now disturbs me – cooked pasta sitting in sauce all day, ready to be reheated in microwaves – but back then it was THE spot to get an early dinner. The most popular pasta by far was penne with a butter chicken sauce. While I never ordered it, my sister and most of my friends were addicted. It wasn't until I was reading a book about pasta by Anna Del Conte – the cook who changed the way the English thought about Italian cooking – that I remembered this dish. Anna had a recipe for 'tortiglioni con pollo al curry', which seemed eerily similar to the dish my sister loved. She talked about Venice being one of the gateways to the spice trade and how those flavours started to seep into some dishes. Shortly after reading Anna's book, Alberto's Lounge, a playful Italian restaurant, opened in Sydney serving 'trippa alla romana', which featured these spices. It was described as 'heading in the direction of butter chicken', and again I was transported back to school days and our local pasta bar.

I decided to give this subcontinental flavour direction a go in the form of a subtly spiced pink pasta sauce. And it was delicious. Unconventional, but delicious. The lesson here is don't knock it until you've tried it.

Serves 4

1 cinnamon stick, broken in half
    to release its flavour
½ teaspoon garam masala
2 cardamom pods, crushed
1 tablespoon salted butter
80 ml (⅓ cup) extra-virgin
    olive oil
2 garlic cloves, finely chopped
3 tablespoons dry white wine
400 g canned whole peeled
    tomatoes
125 ml (½ cup) pouring cream
½ teaspoon caster sugar
sea salt and freshly ground
    black pepper
60 g (1 cup) panko breadcrumbs

FRESH PASTA FOR 4
maccheroni a descita, pici

DRIED PASTA FOR 4
gnocchetti sardi, bucatini

Heat a deep frying pan over medium heat. Throw in the cinnamon, garam masala and cardamom pods and toast for 2 minutes or until fragrant. Add the butter, 1 tablespoon of the olive oil and the garlic, then give everything a good stir for about 30 seconds or until the garlic is soft – you don't want it to burn.

Pour in the white wine and watch it bubble and drink up the flavours for 2 minutes. Add the tomatoes and cream, sprinkle over the sugar and season with salt and pepper. Give everything a big stir, then reduce the heat to low and leave to bubble away for 30 minutes, allowing the spices to imbue their flavours and the sauce to thicken.

Bring a large saucepan of water to a lively boil and season as salty as the sea. Add the pasta and cook until al dente. Drain the pasta, reserving 125 ml (½ cup) of the cooking water.

Heat a small frying pan over medium heat. Add the remaining 3 tablespoons of olive oil and the panko breadcrumbs and cook until golden (don't walk away from the pan as the breadcrumbs only take a few seconds to colour).

When everything is ready, fish out the cinnamon stick and cardamon pods (if you can) and throw in the drained pasta. Give everything a vigorous stir to bring it all together, adding some of your pasta cooking water if needed.

Divide among bowls, shower generously in the breadcrumbs and serve.

Roasted butternut pumpkin, burnt butter, sage

Could there be any greater union than sweet roasted pumpkin, nutty burnt butter and crisp sage? You're more likely to see this starring in ravioli or tortellini, but here I've skipped the effort of making a stuffed pasta and served it up as a pasta sauce. Roasted pumpkin is made to puree, and when thinned out with the butter and pasta cooking water, the texture is much like a rich and creamy carbonara.

Pumpkins are best eaten in season, when they are at their sweetest and most flavoursome. However, even in the height of autumn I've come across a bland and disappointing pumpkin. If you find that your pumpkin still lacks punch after you've tossed it through the butter, a sprinkle of brown sugar will help lift things.

Serves 4

500–600 g butternut pumpkin (about half a whole butternut), peeled and deseeded
1 tablespoon extra-virgin olive oil
sea salt and freshly ground black pepper
½ teaspoon freshly grated nutmeg
125 ml (½ cup) vegetable or chicken stock or water
75 g salted butter
handful of sage leaves
2 tablespoons capers, rinsed, drained and patted dry
handful of grated Parmigiano Reggiano, plus extra to serve

FRESH PASTA FOR 4
farfalle, garganelli

DRIED PASTA FOR 4
conchiglie (shells), farfalle, penne

Preheat the oven to 180°C fan-forced.

Roughly chop the pumpkin into 5 cm pieces. Rub the flesh with the olive oil. Season with salt and the nutmeg and roast for 45–60 minutes, or until very soft and starting to colour. Blitz the pumpkin in a food processor or blender with the stock or water for 1–2 minutes until it has reached a smooth and loose consistency. Set aside.

Place a deep frying pan over medium–low heat. Add the butter to the pan and swirl for 4–5 minutes, or until it starts to turn a golden brown and gives off a nutty aroma. It will get very foamy and start to leave little brown flecks. Add the sage and capers and fry for 2–3 minutes, until crisp. Remove the sage and capers with a slotted spoon and drain on paper towel. Reduce the heat to low. If things are getting too dark, you can add a tablespoon of the water on the boil for the pasta to slow down the cooking. Add the pumpkin puree to your burnt butter and give everything a whisk to incorporate.

Meanwhile, bring a large saucepan of water to a lively boil and season as salty as the sea. Add the pasta and cook until al dente. Drain, reserving 250 ml (1 cup) of the cooking water.

Add the pasta to the pumpkin puree, along with 60 ml (¼ cup) of the pasta cooking water. Toss around to coat the pasta. Add the Parmigiano Reggiano and more cooking water if you feel the sauce needs it.

Serve the pasta with the sage and capers scattered over the top, a grind of black pepper and extra grated Parmigiano Reggiano.

Broccoli and feta ragù

I don't think feta gets the respect it deserves. People are always raving on about the oozy, creamy French cheeses, while I could quite happily indulge in a piece of salty, tangy and crumbly feta. It is incredibly versatile and has the power to transform a simple, one-dimensional dish, just like this broccoli pasta. Usually broccoli pasta is aided by anchovy fillets or sausages, but here it gets a leg up from the feta, which melts into a creamy sauce that coats the pasta. With very few ingredients, it transforms this simple vegetarian meal into a dish any meat eater would enjoy.

Serves 4

1 large head of broccoli
2 tablespoons extra-virgin olive
   oil, plus extra for drizzling
3 garlic cloves, finely chopped
pinch of chilli flakes
sea salt and freshly ground
   black pepper
120 g Greek feta, crumbled
zest of 1 lemon
handful of grated Parmigiano
   Reggiano

FRESH PASTA FOR 4
orecchiette, cavatelli/
malloreddus

DRIED PASTA FOR 4
conchiglie (shells), fusilli

Bring a large saucepan of water to a lively boil and season as salty as the sea.

Peel the broccoli stalk to remove any woody bits, then cut the stalk into 1 cm-thick slices. Chop the florets into 50 cent-sized pieces – you want everything to be around the same size so it cooks evenly. Drop the broccoli into the boiling water and cook for about 3 minutes, until just blanched and bright green. Using a slotted spoon, remove the broccoli and set aside. Keep the water on the boil and add your pasta.

Finely chop the broccoli into small pieces.

Heat the olive oil in a large deep frying pan over medium heat. Add the garlic and cook for about 1 minute, until just starting to turn golden, but please don't let it burn. Add the chilli flakes and broccoli and toss everything together. Season lightly, remembering you have your salty feta and Parmigiano Reggiano to come. Give the mixture another toss.

Ladle 125 ml (½ cup) of the pasta cooking water into the pan and cook, stirring occasionally, for 5 minutes or until the broccoli starts to soften but still has some bite (we don't want a mush). Your finely chopped broccoli should drink up most of this water.

When your pasta is just al dente, use that slotted spoon again to scoop it directly into the sauce. Add the feta and give everything a good stir, adding some more pasta cooking water to loosen it all up. The pasta, broccoli and cheese will drink up a lot of the liquid, so keep this in mind as you're after a loose sauce. Toss the pasta until the feta has all but melted and you are left with a lovely creamy sauce.

Stir through the lemon zest and Parmigiano Reggiano. Give everything a final toss and serve with a drizzle of extra-virgin olive oil.

Pumpkin and cavolo nero lasagne

Lasagne's beauty is more than cheese deep. This beauty lies in the process, pottering away at each step – the pasta, tomato sauce, vegetables, bechamel – to create something truly magical.

There is always room for a quick pasta dish, and you'll find many of them in this book, but don't underestimate the power of taking your time and working your way through a recipe. Everyone seems to confuse complicated with time consuming. Yes, this takes a bit of time, but it's easy and relaxing work. Think of it as a series of easy steps, just like a yoga practice. The size of the baking dish does kind of matter here. You need something that has a 3 litre capacity – I use a dish that's roughly 30 cm by 20 cm with a depth of at least 7 cm.

If you're really feeling like a meat-based lasagne, you could use my bolognese recipe on page 193 and leave out the pumpkin and tomato; just make sure you keep your bol' nice and loose.

Serves 6–8

1 kg pumpkin, peeled, deseeded and cut into 1 cm-thick slices
120 ml extra-virgin olive oil, plus extra for drizzling and greasing
sea salt and freshly ground black pepper
4 garlic cloves, finely chopped
1.2 kg canned whole peeled tomatoes
25 g (½ cup) basil leaves
½ teaspoon caster sugar
1 bunch of cavolo nero, leaves stripped and finely chopped
zest of 1 lemon
250 g mozzarella, grated (or use scamorza – smoked mozzarella)

Bechamel
3 tablespoons cold salted butter
75 g (½ cup) plain flour
650 ml full-cream milk
120 g (1½ cups) finely grated Parmigiano Reggiano
½ teaspoon freshly grated nutmeg
sea salt and freshly ground black pepper

FRESH EGG PASTA DOUGH FOR 4
rolled into 15 sheets,
1.2 mm thick

DRIED PASTA
600 g lasagne sheets

Preheat the oven to 200°C fan-forced.

Brush the pumpkin with 2 tablespoons of the olive oil and season with salt. Place the pumpkin on a baking tray in a single layer and roast for 30–40 minutes, until cooked through and slightly charred at the edges. Depending on your oven, you might find a quick turn of the pumpkin halfway through will ensure even cooking. Remove from the oven and set aside to cool.

Meanwhile, you can get on with your tomato sauce. In a large deep saucepan (tomato sauce always spits when bubbling away and makes a mess), heat 2 tablespoons of the remaining oil over medium heat. Add the garlic and cook for 30 seconds, then pour in the tomatoes, along with basil leaves and sugar. Break up the tomatoes using the back of a wooden spoon, then simmer, stirring from time to time, for 40 minutes, until reduced and thickened. Season to taste.

To make your bechamel, melt the butter in a saucepan over low heat. Add the flour and stir constantly with a wooden spoon for about 2 minutes or until the mixture starts to bubble. This cooks out that raw flour taste. Gradually add the milk, still stirring constantly. If handy, I switch to a whisk to help eliminate as many lumps as I can. Slowly bring to the boil and continue to occasionally stir for 8–10 minutes, until you have a smooth, thick sauce. You're looking for a thickness that passes the 'coat the back of a spoon test', which means dipping your spoon into your bechamel and drawing a finger through it. Does the bechamel wipe clean, leaving an open space through your line? Once it does, remove the pan from the heat and stir through 100 g (1 cup) of the Parmigiano Reggiano, along with the nutmeg. Season with salt and pepper and set aside.

Heat the remaining 2 tablespoons of olive oil in a large frying pan over medium heat and add the cavolo nero. Cook for 5 minutes or until wilted. Add the lemon zest, season with salt and pepper and set aside.

If you're using fresh pasta, I do as Marcella Hazan does and blanch the sheets very quickly. Bring a large saucepan of water to a lively boil and season as salty as the sea. Blanch your lasagne sheets – about three to five at a time to stop them sticking – for no more than 30 seconds, then lay them out on a large sheet of baking paper. Drizzle with olive oil to stop them sticking.

Rub the sides of a 3 litre baking dish with olive oil. Line the base with pasta sheets, trimming if necessary. Spread one-third of the tomato sauce over the pasta. Top with half the pumpkin followed by another layer of pasta, then spread about one-third of the bechamel over the top and evenly sprinkle with half the cavolo nero. Add another layer of pasta, but this time leave some of your pasta overhanging (although you'll have to leave this bit out if using dried lasagne). This helps with the crispy bits, which in my humble opinion is the best part. Add another third of the tomato sauce, the remaining pumpkin, another third of the pasta and bechamel, then top with the remaining cavolo nero and a final layer of pasta (making five in total). You're on the home stretch now. Add the remaining tomato sauce followed by the last of the bechamel. Sprinkle over the mozzarella and remaining Parmigiano Reggiano. Drizzle over some olive oil, making sure you rub it over the overhanging pasta. Bake in the oven for 30–40 minutes, until bubbling, golden and irresistible. Leave to stand for about 10 minutes before serving.

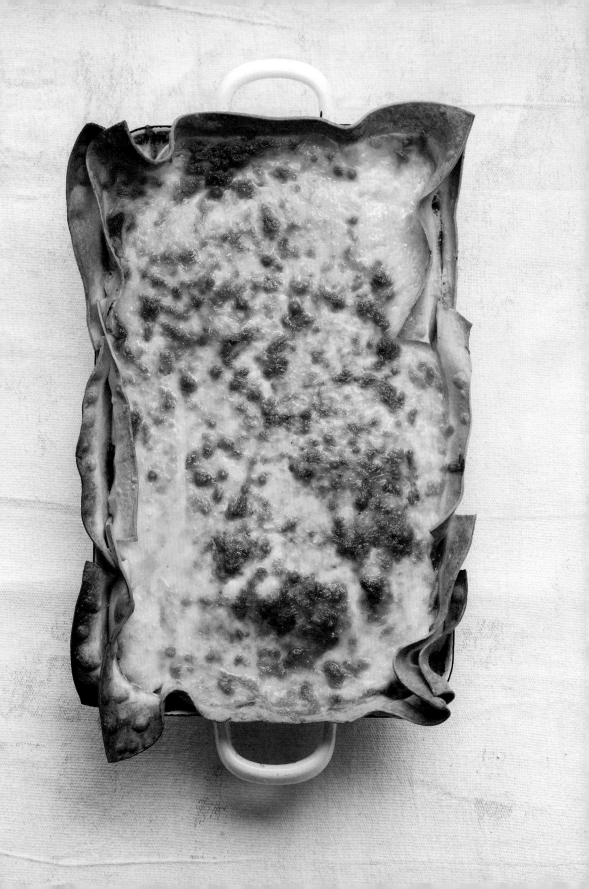

Marinated artichokes, pecorino, dill

I arrived in Rome for pasta school in early spring, when every market, trattoria and roadside van is loaded with crates of globe artichokes. 'Carciofi', as they are called in Italy, can be described as the vegetable of Rome, and while their season in and around Rome is short-lived, artichokes are savoured all over the city – and I mean all over. I enjoyed them fried, stewed, stuffed, braised, roasted and finely shaved raw in punchy salads. At the height of the season, Roman artichokes are marinated to extend their life well after they have disappeared from the markets. There is even a festival that celebrates this humble ingredient – I'm told that artichokes have a strong reputation as an aphrodisiac and can cause debauched sexual revelling, so maybe this is why the season is celebrated so enthusiastically! Either way, I just love how the Italians embrace seasonality with such gusto and white-hot passion. When it's here, it's really here, and it should be enjoyed all the time. We could all take a little away from that.

Here, I've skipped the handling of fresh artichokes – it can get rather hairy – and created a sauce based around the flavours of marinated artichokes. As the inspiration for this dish comes from central Italy, pecorino is my cheese of choice, although Parmigiano Reggiano works just as nicely.

Serves 2

2 tablespoons extra-virgin
  olive oil
2 garlic cloves, finely chopped
1 bird's eye chilli, deseeded and
  finely chopped (use half if you
  prefer less heat)
2 tablespoons baby capers,
  rinsed and drained
170 g marinated artichoke hearts
  in oil, drained and quartered
125 ml (½ cup) dry white wine
zest of 1 lemon
1 tablespoon salted butter
handful of grated pecorino,
  plus extra to serve
3 tablespoons chopped dill
  fronds, plus extra to serve

FRESH PASTA FOR 2
maltagliati, linguine

DRIED PASTA FOR 2
spaghetti

Bring a large saucepan of water to a lively boil and season as salty as the sea. Add the pasta and cook until al dente.

Meanwhile, heat the olive oil in a large frying pan over medium heat. Add the garlic and chilli and sauté for about 1 minute, taking care not to burn the garlic. Throw in the capers, artichoke and white wine and simmer for 5–8 minutes, until the liquid has slightly reduced. Add the lemon zest to give everything a burst of freshness and zing.

Using tongs, fling the pasta directly into the sauce, along with 60 ml (¼ cup) of the cooking water. Add the butter, pecorino and dill fronds and give everything a forceful stir, allowing the sauce to emulsify. Add extra cooking water, 60 ml (¼ cup) at a time, if things look like they need further loosening up.

Divide the pasta between bowls and serve with extra pecorino and dill.

Buffalo mozzarella cream, slow-roasted cherry tomatoes

As you may have worked out by my repetitive Saturday night activity, I am a routine person. It makes me feel grounded and like I may have some control over the world around me, even if it's for just a moment. It won't surprise you, then, that I have a Saturday morning routine, too. Wake up at 6.45 am, tea in bed – earl grey, dash of milk in one of two cups, which is important because my hands fit perfectly around them – with both Forest and Tom. At 7.55 am, we meet our fellow dog-park friends at our local cafe for a coffee – long black with hot milk – then stroll down to the markets by 8.15 am to nab some milk crates and sit in the sun. After breakfast – a Flour and Stone croissant – I slowly do the rounds of the stands. Thanks to our routine, Forest knows which of the stall holders will give him treats. Clever boy.

This recipe is a result of the rounds at the markets. Vannella is a family-run stall selling some incredible soft Italian cheeses. Their buffalo mozzarella is unrivalled and here it makes a sauce that's every bit as seductive as it sounds. Acidic, sweet, rich and creamy. I find making the sauce, with all the mindless repetitive stirring, to be enormously comforting, too. The slow-roasted cherry tomatoes are there to cut through the glorious fat of the sauce by adding a sweet and acidic tone. If you're not inclined to slow-roast them, I suppose you could use some sundried cherry tomatoes; just try to avoid the heavily flavoured cheaper ones from the supermarket deli as I feel they would be overpowering. Like most pasta dishes, this needs to be eaten straight away. Hot pasta and cream pose a serious clumping issue if allowed to sit.

Serves 2

250 g cherry tomatoes, halved
2 garlic cloves, finely sliced
2 tablespoons extra-virgin olive oil, plus extra for drizzling
sea salt and freshly ground black pepper
125 g buffalo mozzarella, roughly chopped, plus the brine from the bag
100 ml pouring cream
1 tablespoon salted butter
handful of grated Parmigiano Reggiano, plus extra to serve

FRESH PASTA FOR 2
farfalle, garganelli

DRIED PASTA FOR 2
farfalle, fusilli, penne, rigatoni

Preheat the oven to 130°C fan-forced.

Place the tomato and garlic on a large baking tray, drizzle over the olive oil and season with salt and pepper. Give everything a good toss around to coat, then arrange the tomato in a single layer, cut-side up.

Roast for 1½–2 hours or until starting to dehydrate. You're looking for a tomato chip.

Place a saucepan over medium heat and add the mozzarella, 2½ tablespoons of the brine from the bag, the cream and butter and stir to melt. Be patient, as the mozzarella takes 15–20 minutes to melt and you'll still be left with a good chunk of the stretched skin. Persevere, stirring frequently, to encourage it to melt through the cream. Discard the residue of cheese that hasn't melted by this stage (there will be some), as it will be rubbery and the flavour will have been sucked into your now creamy and seductive sauce.

Meanwhile, bring a large saucepan of water to a lively boil and season as salty as the sea. Add the pasta and cook until al dente. Using a slotted spoon, add the pasta directly to the sauce, along with 60 ml (¼ cup) of the cooking water and the Parmigiano Reggiano. Stir vigorously to ensure the pasta is well coated.

Divide the pasta between bowls and scatter over the tomato. Drizzle with olive oil and finish with a very light dusting of extra Parmigiano Reggiano and pepper. Eat straight away.

Mixed mushrooms, optional bacon crumb

The bacon crumb is optional because, quite honestly, this dish is delicious with just the mushrooms. I do call for mixed mushrooms because they all bring different flavours and textures. It's relatively easy to buy mixed mushrooms these days – they sell packs of them in the supermarket – but if there are only button mushrooms available then that's just fine; it will still be delicious. But do promise me one thing: never wash your mushrooms. They are little sponges and will soak up the water, which will only dilute their flavour. To clean, give them a wipe with paper towel or a pastry brush. Oh, and if you can't find crème fraîche, then sour cream works, too.

Serves 2

300 g mixed mushrooms (such as button, cup, oyster, swiss brown, portobello or enoki)
2 tablespoons salted butter
1 tablespoon extra-virgin olive oil
1 garlic clove, finely chopped
1 tablespoon thyme leaves
3 tablespoons dry white wine or chicken or vegetable stock
sea salt and freshly ground black pepper
2 tablespoons crème fraîche
1 lemon
grated Parmigiano Reggiano, to serve

Bacon crumb (optional)
1 tablespoon extra-virgin olive oil
1 bacon rasher, finely chopped
40 g (½ cup) fresh breadcrumbs

FRESH PASTA FOR 2
pappardelle, reginette (mafaldine), fettuccine

DRIED PASTA FOR 2
fettuccine

If you choose to make the bacon crumb, heat a small frying pan over medium heat. Add the olive oil and bacon and sauté for about 5 minutes, until starting to crisp. Add the breadcrumbs and continue to sauté, stirring frequently, for 5–6 minutes, until everything is a deep golden brown. Transfer to a small bowl and leave to cool.

Wipe the mushrooms with paper towel to remove any dirt. Rip any large mushrooms in half and leave the smaller ones whole.

Melt the butter in a large frying pan over medium heat. Add the olive oil, garlic and thyme and cook for 1–2 minutes, until fragrant.

Add the mushrooms and the wine or stock and continue to cook for another minute or until the liquid comes to the boil. Season with salt and pepper.

Turn off the heat and stir in the crème fraîche. Zest in the lemon and add a good squeeze of the juice.

Bring a large saucepan of water to a lively boil and season as salty as the sea. Add the pasta and cook until al dente. Drain, reserving 125 ml (½ cup) of the cooking water, then tip the pasta into your mushroom mixture, giving the pan a good swish around.

Add some of the pasta cooking water if the sauce is too thick, then season with salt and pepper.

Divide the pasta between bowls and serve with Parmigiano Reggiano and the bacon crumb (if using) showered over the top.

Ricotta, spinach, black pepper

Don't even try and use low-fat ricotta here. For me, this is impossible and I refuse to even acknowledge its existence. We're dealing with so few ingredients here that you should invest in the good stuff. Buy fresh ricotta from your local deli. The one that has texture and wobble.

Serves 4

2 tablespoons salted butter
75 g (1½ cups) baby spinach leaves
375 g fresh full-fat ricotta
sea salt and freshly ground
    black pepper
zest of 1 lemon
handful of grated Parmigiano
    Reggiano
freshly grated nutmeg, to serve

FRESH PASTA FOR 4
paccheri, busiate, garganelli

DRIED PASTA FOR 4
fusilli, penne, rigatoni

Bring a large saucepan of water to a lively boil and season as salty as the sea. Add the pasta and cook until al dente.

Melt the butter in a frying pan over medium heat and add the spinach leaves.

When the spinach leaves start to wilt, crumble in the ricotta with a pinch of salt and a really generous grinding of pepper. Add the lemon zest, then remove from the heat.

Drain the pasta, reserving about 250 ml (1 cup) of the cooking water. Toss the pasta through the ricotta and spinach, adding half the cooking water to loosen things up. You want it to be on the wetter side, as the pasta and cheese absorb a lot of liquid and you don't want it going dry. Add a little more cooking water if needed. Stir through the Parmigiano Reggiano and a grating of nutmeg and serve.

Anchovy, garlic, capers, green olives

Essentially, this sauce is puttancesa bianco – Napoli's famed pasta dish but without the tomato. Spaghetti puttanesca translates to 'spaghetti in the style of prostitutes' and there are almost as many stories about the origin of this dish as there are ways to make it. My favourite is that the pungent aromas of the anchovy, garlic and olives tossed through the pasta were how the Neapolitan prostitutes lured customers to their doors. Another, based on the fact that this dish can be made entirely with ingredients kept in your pantry, is that it was made by prostitutes for a quick meal, in between their engagements.

The traditional recipe uses tomatoes, which you are welcome to add. I prefer canned tomatoes – add one 400 g can of whole peeled tomatoes after the capers and olives and cook for an extra 10–15 minutes. Either route, this dish is a kick, punch and a pow of flavours, which I suppose is why it was the dish of choice for Neapolitan ladies of the night.

Serves 2

3 tablespoons extra-virgin
  olive oil
40 g (½ cup) fresh breadcrumbs
pinch of chilli flakes
sea salt
6 anchovy fillets
3 garlic cloves, chopped
3 tablespoons baby capers,
  rinsed and drained
60 g (⅓ cup) pitted green
  Sicilian olives, finely chopped
3 oregano sprigs, leaves picked
zest of 1 lemon

FRESH PASTA FOR 2
pici, linguine

DRIED PASTA FOR 2
bucatini, spaghetti

Heat a large frying pan over medium heat. Add 2 tablespoons of the olive oil, the breadcrumbs, chilli flakes and a pinch of salt. Sauté for 3–5 minutes, until the breadcrumbs are golden and crisp, then remove from the pan and set aside. This will be your garnish.

Bring a large saucepan of water to a lively boil and season moderately (you have plenty of salt in the sauce). Add the pasta and cook until molto al dente (see page 89), reserving 125 ml (½ cup) of the cooking water. We're going to finish the pasta in the sauce so ensure it still has that all-important bite. If you decide to add a can of tomatoes to your sauce, get the sauce going before you cook the pasta.

Return the frying pan to the stovetop and set over low heat. Add the remaining 1 tablespoon of olive oil and the anchovy fillets and slowly sauté for about 1 minute, until the anchovies start to dissolve. Add the garlic and sauté for another minute – you want to soften the garlic, but take care not to burn it. Add the capers and olives and sauté for 2 minutes – the smell should be intoxicating. You can add tomatoes at this point if you desire. If so, cook the sauce for a further 10–15 minutes, until reduced and thickened.

Using tongs, transfer your cooked pasta directly to the sauce, along with the oregano leaves and lemon zest. Toss everything together with a firm hand. If the sauce needs further loosening, add a splash of the pasta cooking water. Cook, stirring, for about 1 minute, until everything is nicely combined, then remove from the heat.

Divide the pasta between bowls and serve with the chilli-spiked breadcrumbs showered over the top.

Garlic, chilli, parsley, optional seafood

For me, this is the most festive pasta dish Italy has. With its red and green confetti speckled through the pasta, it looks like someone has opened a Christmas cracker over the top. And then there is the magic simplicity of it all. Despite the small number of ingredients, it's packed full of flavour and quite happily satisfies me even at the hungriest of times.

If I'm after something a little showier, though, this dish is a great canvas for a topping of seafood. Here, I've used yabbies as I feel they give it a uniquely Australian flair, but prawns, calamari, crab and even fish fillets also work beautifully.

If you're using crab, fold it through the pasta at the last minute with a squeeze of lemon. For the other varieties of seafood, you can either cook them in the garlic and chilli mixture and finish with a squeeze of lemon, or grill them separately and adorn the pasta at the table.

Serves 4

125 ml (½ cup) extra-virgin olive oil
4 garlic cloves, finely sliced
1 teaspoon chilli flakes (use half if you prefer less heat)
15 g (½ cup) chopped flat-leaf parsley leaves
zest of 1 lemon and juice of ½

Optional add-ons
12 small peeled and deveined yabbies or uncooked prawns, 225 g fresh crab meat, 275 g roughly chopped calamari or 300 g roughly chopped skinless, boneless white fish fillets, such as red mullet
3 tablespoons dry white wine
sea salt

FRESH PASTA FOR 4
tagliolini

DRIED PASTA FOR 4
angel hair, linguine, spaghetti

Bring a large saucepan of water to a lively boil and season as salty as the sea. This is an important step, as the sauce itself doesn't have salt, so we need to ensure the pasta is well seasoned. Add the pasta and cook until al dente.

Meanwhile, place a frying pan over low heat and add the olive oil, garlic and chilli. Cook for 2–3 minutes or until the garlic becomes lightly golden and soft. The smell will be uplifting and it will look bright and vivid. Do not let it brown and ruin your mood.

If you are adding seafood, throw in the yabbies or prawns, calamari or fish now, along with the white wine to stop the garlic burning. The cooking times will vary depending on what seafood you use, but generally 3–5 minutes should be long enough. If you're not adding seafood, proceed to the next step.

Drain the pasta and toss it through the sauce, along with the parsley, lemon zest and a squeeze of lemon juice, ensuring you coat every last strand. Taste, and if necessary, season with salt.

If you went with crab, you can toss it through now.

Transfer the pasta to a large serving bowl or individual bowls and serve.

Calamari, tomato, black olive ragù

A tomato-based pasta sauce can do no wrong, and here it's met with the unexpected combination of calamari and olives, all of which are cooked down to a ragù-like sauce. To the unknowing eye, this ragù might fool one into thinking they are eating meat, which often happens at OTTO, the upmarket Sydney-based Italian restaurant that inspired this sauce. OTTO has been serving their strozzapreti, king prawn, black olive, chilli, tomato and calamari pasta for 20 years. It's well and truly cemented as a signature dish that's loved by their fiercely loyal diners. At one point, the restaurant tried to remove it from the menu and there was a complete uproar, so much so that the dish came back and has since never left. The sauce is simple in its execution, but it does require some cooking time to allow the calamari to soften. OTTO adds prawns to the final dish, which I've left out, but of course feel free to add them if you're feeling fancy. Fish sauce may sound like an unusual addition, but I do as I'm told by OTTO's chef Richard Ptacnik – and he's right, it adds a rich umami-ness that's hard to match.

Ask your fishmonger to clean the calamari. If you buy it whole, gently pull out the legs and backbone. Reserve the legs but discard the eyes and beak.

Serves 4

2 tablespoons extra-virgin
  olive oil
1 garlic clove, finely chopped
1 small leek, finely chopped
200 g calamari, cleaned and
  very finely chopped
125 ml (½ cup) dry white wine
  (one that's good enough to
  drink and enjoy with the dish)
400 g tomato passata
1 bird's eye chilli, finely chopped,
  plus extra to serve (use half
  if you prefer less heat)
1 tablespoon Thai fish sauce
35 g black olives, pitted and
  finely chopped

FRESH PASTA FOR 4
paccheri, calamarata (basically
paccheri cut into the size of
calamari rings)

DRIED PASTA FOR 4
conchiglie (shells),
penne, rigatoni

Heat a heavy-based saucepan over medium heat. Add the olive oil, garlic and leek and sauté for 2 minutes or until things start to soften but not colour. Add the calamari (it will release lots of liquid) and continue to cook, stirring, for about 5 minutes, until the excess liquid from the calamari has evaporated.

Add the white wine to deglaze the pan and cook until the liquid has again evaporated – another 5 minutes or so.

Add the passata and chilli and give everything a good stir. Rinse your passata jar with 60 ml (¼ cup) of water and pour that in, too. Finally, add the fish sauce. Now it's time to let it do its thing. Reduce the heat to low, put a lid on and leave to cook for 2 hours, checking and stirring occasionally to make sure the sauce doesn't burn on the bottom of the pan.

Bring a large saucepan of water to a lively boil and season as salty as the sea. Add the pasta and cook until al dente, reserving 125 ml (½ cup) of the cooking water.

When ready to serve, add the olives to the ragù and stir through. Add the pasta directly to the pan, along with some of the cooking water if needed to loosen up the ragù, and give everything a good stir.

Divide among bowls. No to serving with cheese but yes to serving with extra chilli.

Smoked trout, lemon cream, pink peppercorns

I usually use smoked eel in this dish, but I know it rubs some people up the wrong way, which is why I've opted to use smoked trout here instead. I'm not talking about slices of smoked trout, I'm talking about the whole fillets that you can flake. The smokiness of the fish paired with the tangy lemon cream is heightened by those pretty little pink peppercorns that make this a real showstopper of a dish, despite taking a mere six steps to make. Pink peppercorns are actually a spice and they bring a warm peppery heat, along with a sweet citrus aroma. Of course, these aren't a necessity and black pepper is a perfectly acceptable substitute. And while I'm going, you could even remove the fish, too, to turn this into pasta al limone, a true Italian classic for very good reason.

Serves 2

zest and juice of 1 lemon, plus
   a little extra juice to serve
150 ml pouring cream
2 tablespoons salted butter
150–200 g smoked trout or eel
sea salt
1 teaspoon pink peppercorns,
   crushed

FRESH PASTA FOR 2
tagliatelle, tagliolini

DRIED PASTA FOR 2
angel hair, linguine, spaghetti

Bring a large saucepan of water to a lively boil and season as salty as the sea. Add the pasta and cook until molto al dente (see page 89).

Place the lemon zest, lemon juice and cream in a saucepan over medium heat. Cook for about 2 minutes or until the cream starts to simmer – don't let it boil. Reduce the heat to low.

Whisk in half the butter until melted, then add the other half. Keep stirring until everything comes together and the sauce is lovely and creamy. Remove from the heat and flake in the smoked fish. Taste and season with salt.

Scoop out 125 ml (½ cup) of the pasta cooking water as a backup – you shouldn't need any extra liquid, but it's a good precaution to take.

Using tongs, pull your pasta directly into the lemon cream, allowing some cooking water to come along with the pasta. Give everything a good stir and add some of the reserved cooking water if needed.

Divide the pasta between bowls and sprinkle over the peppercorns for a fancy finish, along with a little extra lemon juice.

Mussels, roasted cherry tomatoes, fennel

Mussel shells are the perfect vessel to catch fregola or other small pasta shapes. Here, I've cooked them alongside a zesty, sticky sauce of cherry tomatoes, fennel, preserved lemon and harissa. At the end, I toss through the cooked fregola, which plump up in the mussel sauce with a succulence that only pasta can do. Pipis or clams work well here as a substitute for the mussels and, in fact, you could even grill some calamari or prawns, too.

Serves 2 generously

2 tablespoons extra-virgin olive oil
2 garlic cloves, finely chopped
250 g cherry tomatoes
1 small fennel, chopped, fronds reserved
1 teaspoon harissa
2 preserved lemon quarters, skin only, finely sliced
125 ml (½ cup) dry white wine
1 kg mussels, scrubbed and debearded (if you have any mussels that are open, give them a tap; discard any that do not close)
zest of 1 lemon
crusty bread, to serve

FRESH PASTA FOR 2
fregola

DRIED PASTA FOR 2
ditalini, fregola, risoni

Place a large deep frying pan with a lid over medium heat. Add the olive oil and garlic and sauté for 30 seconds, then add the tomatoes, fennel, harissa and preserved lemon. Give everything a stir and cook for 5 minutes. Add the wine and let it bubble away for about a minute. Reduce the heat to medium–low, then cover and leave to cook, stirring occasionally, for 15–20 minutes.

Bring a large saucepan of water to a lively boil and season as salty as the sea. Add the pasta and cook until molto al dente (see page 89).

Back to the sauce. Increase the heat to medium, arrange the mussels over the top of the sauce and cover. Cook for 5–10 minutes, until the mussels open. Some might take slightly longer and if this is the case, remove the opened mussels so they don't overcook. Discard any unopened mussels.

Drain the pasta and add it to the pan, along with any open mussels you took out. Give everything a big stir and remove from the heat, then scatter over the lemon zest and reserved fennel fronds.

Serve straight from the pan, with bread on the side to mop up the juice.

Clams, fermented chilli, lemon, toasted garlic

This is what everyone came for right? Surely there is no better combination than the brininess of clams, the zestiness of lemon and the fire of chilli. While this dish does not need any adaptations, I was inspired by my local pizzeria to use fermented chilli and toasted garlic as another expression. If you've eaten Bella Brutta's clam pizza in Sydney you'll know what I'm talking about. The fermented chilli here comes in the form of sambal oelek, an Indonesian chilli paste, but purists can use fresh chilli or chilli flakes if this is a step too far away from the classic. For me, it's simply another way of celebrating this killer combination.

I actually prefer to use a dried pasta in this dish, and in fact most olive oil–driven sauces like the firmness of dried pasta, but if you do use fresh – which I have done many times – just let your pasta dry out for a short while (no more than an hour) to give it a little extra bite.

Serves 2

500 g clams
3 tablespoons extra-virgin
   olive oil
3 large garlic cloves, finely
   chopped
1 tablespoon salted butter
1 tablespoon sambel oelek (use
   half if you prefer less heat)
75 ml dry white wine
small bunch of flat-leaf parsley,
   leaves picked and roughly
   chopped
zest of 1 lemon and juice of ½

FRESH PASTA FOR 2
linguine, tagliolini

DRIED PASTA FOR 2
linguine, spaghetti

Place the clams in a large bowl and cover with cold water. Set aside for 1 hour to purge them of any sand and grit. Drain.

Bring a large saucepan of water to a lively boil and season as salty as the sea. Add the pasta and cook until al dente.

Meanwhile, heat the olive oil with the garlic in a large frying pan over low heat, until starting to warm – not hot, do you hear me? Garlic burns fast and if you add it to already-hot oil, the outside will brown before the inside has had a chance to cook. Cook, stirring constantly and keeping an eye on it, for about 5 minutes or until fragrant and beginning to colour. Add the butter, along with the sambal oelek, and allow to melt.

Add the drained clams and increase the heat to medium. Pour in the wine, then cover and leave for 2 minutes or until most of the clams have opened.

Drain the pasta and add it to the opened clams. Discard any clams that have not opened. Toss well and leave for a minute, then stir through the parsley, lemon zest and juice.

Transfer to a big serving bowl and dig in.

Prawns, tomato, pistachio

Prawn bisque used to seem so cheffy and not something I'd do at home until someone actually talked me through it. In its basic form, it's terribly easy, uses up the prawn heads and shells, and boy does it add flavour to a pasta sauce. I know it increases the cooking time to this sauce, well 20 minutes or so, but really if you're cooking this on a Saturday, it shouldn't be a hassle.

As you're making a stock from the prawn heads, you do want to be particular about where you get them from. Choose fresh or snap frozen.

Serves 4

500 g unpeeled raw prawns
3 tablespoons extra-virgin olive
   oil, plus extra for drizzling
1 small carrot, roughly chopped
1 celery stalk, roughly chopped
1 small onion, roughly chopped
100 ml dry white wine
1 tablespoon tomato paste
sea salt and freshly ground
   black pepper
1 garlic clove, finely chopped
2 teaspoons chopped oregano
   leaves, plus extra to serve
pinch of chilli flakes (optional)
300 g cherry tomatoes, halved,
   or roma tomatoes, chopped
zest of 1 lemon
unsalted chopped pistachios,
   lightly toasted, to serve

FRESH PASTA FOR 4
busiate, linguine, tagliatelle

DRIED PASTA FOR 4
fettuccine, fusilli, linguine

Clean the prawns by chopping off their heads and removing the shells – keep everything, as this will be the base of your prawn stock, which will enrich the sauce. Devein the prawns – I use a toothpick to help with this.

Heat a large saucepan over medium heat. Add 1 tablespoon of the olive oil, along with the carrot, celery and onion, and cook for 5 minutes or until soft. Throw in the prawn shells and heads. Using the back of a wooden spoon, crush the heads to draw out all the flavour, then cook for 3–5 minutes, until the prawn shells change colour. Add the wine and leave it to boil and bubble for 2 minutes. Add the tomato paste and a pinch of salt, along with 1 litre of water. Reduce the heat to low and leave it to simmer away for 15 minutes.

Strain the prawn stock into a jug, discarding the prawn shells and heads and vegetables. This is now a lovely, flavour-packed stock that's ready to boost your pasta sauce. Keep warm.

Place a frying pan over medium heat. Add the remaining 2 tablespoons of olive oil, the garlic, oregano and chilli (if using) and cook for about 30 seconds, until fragrant. Add the tomato and season with salt and pepper. Give everything a good toss around and leave to cook for 15 minutes or until the tomato is soft and has released its juice. Add 125 ml (½ cup) of your prawn stock, then leave to cook for another 5 minutes to allow the flavours to come together. The remaining stock will keep in the fridge for 3 days or in the freezer for up to 3 months (just remember to label it in the freezer; if you're anything like me, you'll forget what it is).

Throw the prawns into the pan and cook for 3–5 minutes, until their little blue bodies blush pink.

Meanwhile, bring a large saucepan of water to a lively boil and season as salty as the sea. Add the pasta and cook until al dente.

Using tongs, add the pasta directly to the sauce, along with the lemon zest. Give the pan a really big shake and stir to bring everything together.

Divide the pasta among bowls, ensuring there is even prawn distribution (people get very upset) and scatter over the pistachios. Drizzle over a little olive oil and finish with a few oregano leaves for prettiness.

Crab, sweetcorn, chilli

I went to university in the country. The town was mostly dominated by university students except for one weekend in October, when the population would swell for the Bathurst 1000, a V8 motorcar race that circled Mount Panorama. Like every good Aussie country town, there was a family-run Chinese restaurant on the main strip. Enjoying university life to the fullest, Happy's Chinese would be my Sunday night recovery dinner. Their sweetcorn and crab noodle soup (I'm only now questioning the freshness of the crab considering the town is more than 200 km from the ocean) had extraordinary curative powers after a big night out.

Of course, the only thing I'm pulling from this story is the combination of corn and crab (I'm glad to have those days behind me), as the sweetness of both pair very nicely. Then there's the bright colour of the sweetcorn, which is so joyful to look at. Tossed through egg pasta and finished with butter, chilli and chives, this pasta also has healing powers for the soul.

Serves 4

2 tablespoons extra-virgin olive oil
4 spring onions, finely sliced
2 garlic cloves, finely chopped
1 bird's eye chilli, finely chopped (optional or only add half if you prefer less heat)
2 large or 3 small sweetcorn cobs, husks removed, kernels sliced off
sea salt
1 tablespoon salted butter
225 g fresh crab meat
zest and juice of 1 lemon
1 bunch of chives, finely snipped

FRESH PASTA FOR 4
linguine, tagliolini

DRIED PASTA FOR 4
angel hair, linguine, spaghetti

Heat 1 tablespoon of the olive oil in a large frying pan over medium heat. Add the spring onion, garlic and chilli (if using) and cook for 2 minutes or until soft but not brown. Add the sweetcorn kernels, along with 500 ml (2 cups) of water. Season with salt. Cook for 30 minutes or until the sweetcorn is bright yellow, soft and creamy, adding a dash more water if things start to dry up along the way. It will smell almost buttery.

Meanwhile, bring a large saucepan of water to a lively boil and season as salty as the sea. Add the pasta and cook until al dente.

Tip the sweetcorn mixture and 60 ml (¼ cup) of pasta cooking water into a blender or food processor and blitz for at least 2 minutes to create a smooth yellow puree. You're looking for a pourable puree, so feel free to add more pasta cooking water if you feel it needs it. Season with salt.

Wipe out the frying pan, then add the butter and return the pan to medium heat. When the butter is melted and foaming, pour in your corn puree and reduce the heat to low.

Drain the pasta, reserving 250 ml (1 cup) of the cooking water.

Throw the pasta into your corn puree, along with half of the reserved cooking water. Give the mixture a strong stir to bring everything together, adding more cooking water if you need to loosen things up. Finally, stir through the crab, the lemon zest and juice and half the chives.

Divide the pasta among bowls, scatter over the remaining chives and serve immediately.

Chicken gravy, crisp brussels sprouts

This is the pasta dish I make every time I want to transport myself back to my year in Piedmont. A meat sauce, almost gravy-like, left over from the famed 'bollito misto' (translated literally as mixed boiled meats) is tossed through pasta, most likely agnolotti del plin (filled with the left-over meat from the bollito misto). You'll find it at most restaurants in the region and this left-over meat gravy is one of the things I miss most about Italy. Even so, I can't say I'm driven to cook bollito misto at home. I was never one to enjoy the offal that would inevitably get dispersed through the collection of mixed meats. Each meat had such a different texture that it was quite confronting when served as is with some salsa verde. But the sauce, now that stuff was liquid gold.

One day I had the most extraordinary revelation and it was this: I could roast a chicken (or a bunch of thighs) for their juices and sauce, as long as I could find another use for the actual meat. This is easy enough with chicken: sandwiches, salads, pies or a quick weeknight curry (and if you felt like it, you could finely chop the chicken and toss it through the pasta, too). I set about cooking the chicken just for its gravy and the end result, tossed through eggy pasta, took me right back to the streets of Piedmont and my ultimate comfort food. It's become the dish that gives me a hug when the world does not.

This recipe is really driven by the quality of your chicken stock, so either use a homemade one or purchase some from a butcher. I've finished the dish with some crispy brussels sprouts, but roasted greens like cavolo nero and kale work well – just make sure you get them crisp.

158

Serves 4

500 g chicken thighs, skin on
    and bone in (roughly 4 thighs)
2 tablespoons salted butter
2 tablespoons extra-virgin
    olive oil
1 garlic clove, skin on, lightly
    smashed with the side of
    a knife
1 rosemary sprig
85 ml dry white wine
125 ml (½ cup) good-quality
    chicken stock
sea salt and freshly ground
    black pepper
handful of brussels sprouts
    (or use 4 large cavolo nero
    or kale leaves)
2 teaspoons plain flour
handful of grated Parmigiano
    Reggiano, plus extra to serve

FRESH PASTA FOR 4
garganelli, tagliatelle

DRIED PASTA FOR 4
rigatoni, penne,
conchiglie (shells)

Preheat the oven to 200°C fan-forced.

Remove the bones from the chicken and chop the meat into 3 cm cubes. Heat half the butter and 1 tablespoon of the olive oil in a large deep frying pan with a lid over medium–high heat. When the butter has melted, add the garlic and rosemary and swirl them around in the pan for 30 seconds. Add the chicken, along with the bones, and cook for 10–15 minutes or until starting to brown and the fat renders out.

Add the wine and let it bubble away for about 2 minutes or until you can stop smelling the booze. Add the chicken stock and use a wooden spoon to scrape the sticky chickeny bits off the base of the pan. Season with salt and pepper, then put the lid on, reduce the heat to low and cook for 20 minutes.

Meanwhile, remove the ends from the sprouts so you can pull the leaves apart. Place the leaves on a baking tray, toss through the remaining 1 tablespoon of olive oil and season with salt. Spread the leaves so they have plenty of room to crisp up (they'll go soggy if they are bunched together). Bake for 15–20 minutes, until slightly burnt and crisp. Remove from the oven and set aside. Do not cover as they'll lose their crispness. If you are using cavolo nero or kale, tear up the leaves, coat in olive oil and bake for 5–10 minutes, until crisp and golden.

Remove the chicken, bones, garlic and rosemary from the pan. Set the chicken aside for something else and discard the bones, garlic and rosemary. You should be left with some lovely juices in the pan. Whisk in the remaining butter and the flour and cook for 1–2 minutes, until starting to thicken. Turn off the heat and cover to keep warm while you cook your pasta.

Bring a large saucepan of water to a lively boil and season as salty as the sea. Add the pasta and cook until al dente. Drain and add the pasta directly to your gravy sauce. Add the Parmigiano Reggiano and give everything a toss.

Divide the pasta among bowls and serve with the crisp brussels sprout leaves (or cavolo nero or kale leaves) and extra cheese scattered over the top.

Chicken meatballs, tomato and lemon broth

Yes this does require a few steps – make the meatballs, boil the meatballs, then bring it all together in a crazy flavour-packed broth – but it's all simple, pleasurable work that fits in nicely with the SNP concept. These chicken meatballs are lovely and springy, helped along by the fact that they're boiled rather than fried. Sometimes I serve them over a can of drained cannellini beans and greens for a non-pasta meal.

Serves 4

500–700 ml chicken stock
2 tablespoons extra-virgin olive
   oil, plus extra for drizzling
2 garlic cloves, finely chopped
1 bird's eye chilli, roughly
   chopped (use half if you
   prefer less heat)
250 g cherry tomatoes
125 ml (½ cup) dry white wine
sea salt and freshly ground
   black pepper
zest of 1 lemon
30 g (1 cup) flat-leaf parsley
   leaves, roughly chopped

Chicken meatballs

500 g chicken mince
80 g (1 cup) finely grated
   Parmigiano Reggiano,
   plus extra to serve
1 small egg, lightly beaten
1 tablespoon thyme leaves
zest of 1 lemon
sea salt and freshly ground
   black pepper

FRESH PASTA FOR 4
cavatelli/malloreddus

DRIED PASTA FOR 4
risoni, ditalini, cavatelli
or any small-shaped pasta

To make the chicken meatballs, combine the chicken mince, Parmigiano Reggiano, egg, thyme, lemon zest and a generous pinch of salt and pepper in a bowl. Squish everything together with your hands to combine well. Using a teaspoon as a guide, roll the mixture into bite-sized meatballs, keeping your hands wet to avoid the mixture sticking as you roll. Patience is key here. Take your time to keep all the meatballs small and roughly the same size, as they pair better with the pasta. The meatballs can be kept in the fridge for up to 3 days.

Bring the stock to a gentle simmer in a saucepan over medium heat. Working in batches, add the meatballs and poach for 5 minutes or until they float to the surface like little buoys. Remove with a slotted spoon and set aside, reserving the stock.

Place a deep frying pan over medium heat and add the olive oil, garlic and chilli. Sauté for 1 minute or until fragrant, but not brown. Add the cherry tomatoes and sauté for a further minute.

Pour in the wine and cook for 5 minutes or until it starts to bubble away. Add about 300 ml of the reserved chicken stock and cook for 10 minutes or until the tomatoes are soft. Season with salt and pepper.

Meanwhile, bring a large saucepan of water to a lively boil and season as salty as the sea. Add the pasta and cook until al dente, then drain.

Add the meatballs to the sauce, along with the cooked pasta and the lemon zest and toss everything together.

Divide the pasta among bowls and serve with a good drizzle of olive oil, the parsley and a grating of Parmigiano Reggiano.

Chicken and mortadella agnolotti del plin

Agnolotti del plin hails from Piedmont, where I lived for a year. This meat-filled pasta was one of the first dishes I ate upon my arrival, and the dish I continued to eat at every opportunity throughout the year. 'Plin' means 'pinch' in Piedmontese dialect and it's this movement that I find most satisfying. Traditionally, the agnolotti are filled with the left-over meats from another local dish, bollito misto, and served in the flavoursome broth from the boiled meats (see page 158). I'll often fail to go the whole hog and skip to something more approachable, such as this chicken and mortadella combo. Scott Williams, a friend and one of the best pasta chefs I know, gave me this filling recipe and, truthfully, it sits better with the Australian weather. I know that making filled pasta can be a little daunting but, really, this one is just a fold, trim, pinch and cut.

If your stock is lacking richness, you can brown the butter before adding the stock. It will give your sauce a deeper flavour.

Every time I enjoy agnolotti – made traditionally or not – it transports me back to the streets of Bra and to that magical year of really living.

Serves 4 (or 2 greedy people)

250 g chicken mince
150 g sliced mortadella
60 g (¾ cup) grated Parmigiano
  Reggiano, plus extra to serve
3 tablespoons finely
  snipped chives
1 egg
sea salt and freshly ground
  black pepper
Tipo 00 flour, for dusting
250 ml (1 cup) good-quality
  chicken stock
3 tablespoons salted butter,
  roughly chopped
about 10 sage leaves

FRESH EGG PASTA DOUGH FOR 4

Place the chicken mince, mortadella, Parmigiano Reggiano, chives, egg and a generous pinch of salt and pepper in a food processor. Blitz for about 2 minutes, until you have a well-combined filling, then set aside in the fridge while you make your pasta. Friends, this filling can be made up to 2 days ahead.

The key to successful stuffed pasta is to keep your pasta really fresh so it seals itself, so it's best to work in batches to prevent the dough from drying out. Follow the instructions for rolling out the dough on page 38, until your pasta is 1 mm thick.

Lay a pasta sheet on a lightly floured work surface with a long edge facing you. Along the centre of the sheet, dot evenly spaced half teaspoon pieces of filling, keeping them roughly 3 cm apart. See overleaf for a visual guide.

Your pasta should be sticky enough, but if you find that it has dried out a bit, dip your finger in water and run it along the top edge of the dough to moisten it, which will help it stick together.

Fold the bottom edge of the pasta over the filling and seal, taking care to squeeze out any air as you press along the top. With a long sheet of pasta like this, I find it easier to do this working from right to left, or left to right, to ensure that the sheet evenly reaches over the filling.

Trim the top edge of the folded pasta about 5 mm–1 cm above the filling, preferably using a fluted pastry cutter for a pretty, frilly edge to neaten things up.

Now that your filling is neatly covered, here comes the 'plin' part. Pinch either side of the filling using both your forefingers and thumbs, much like a crab-claw pincer movement, ensuring that you remove any air. Work your way down the line, pinching between all the fillings. Pinch, pinch, pinch. See, while it's delicate work, it's very satisfying.

To finish things off, using your fluted pastry cutter at a 45 degree angle and with a bit of force, quickly cut between each agnolotti to separate them. The rolling motion almost folds the agnolotti over, creating little pockets to cup your lovely broth.

Spread out your agnolotti in a single layer on a well-floured work surface. Whatever you do, don't let them touch or they will stick together. Repeat until you run out of dough and filling.

Bring a large saucepan of water to a lively boil and season as salty as the sea. Drop your agnolotti into the rapid bubbles.

Place the stock, butter and sage leaves in a large deep frying pan over high heat and bring to the boil. When your pasta is almost cooked and the agnolotti have risen to the surface, scoop them directly into your simmering sauce.

Give everything a good swirl to emulsify the sauce and coat each and every agnolotti. Transfer to a large serving bowl and serve in the middle of the table with a healthy amount of Parmigiano Reggiano and a good grind of pepper.

Notes: This also makes a great filling for other stuffed pastas.

The agnolotti can be frozen. Simply lay out on a tray to freeze and, once frozen, seal in a zip-lock bag. They can then be cooked from frozen – just add an extra minute or two to the cooking time.

Chicken and clove ragù, lemon breadcrumbs

This is the perfect summertime ragù. It follows the same slow and gentle cooking principles that all ragùs require, but the result is light and zesty, yet satisfying, in the only way a ragù can be. This 'white' ragù (which means no tomato) is enhanced by the addition of cloves and anchovy fillets – but fear not anchovy-phobes, this doesn't give it a fishy flavour. They are simply there for their umami punch. Like all ragùs, this can be made ahead and reheated on the day. In fact, a day-old ragù will have more depth of flavour. The panko breadcrumbs add another dimension to this dish, but they are optional if you simply can't be bothered.

Serves 4

80 ml (⅓ cup) extra-virgin
  olive oil
1 small carrot, finely chopped
  or grated
1 celery stalk, finely chopped
½ small onion, finely chopped
3 garlic cloves, finely chopped
sea salt
4 anchovy fillets
500 g chicken mince
3 cloves
2 fresh or dried bay leaves
6 thyme sprigs
freshly ground black pepper
250 ml (1 cup) dry white wine
375 ml (1½ cups) chicken stock
30 g (½ cup) panko breadcrumbs
zest of 1 lemon
75 g (1½ cups) baby spinach leaves
1 tablespoon salted butter
grated Parmigiano Reggiano,
  to serve

FRESH PASTA FOR 4
reginette (mafaldine), paccheri, pappardelle, tagliatelle

DRIED PASTA FOR 4
conchiglie (shells), fusilli, rigatoni

Heat a large deep flameproof casserole dish over medium heat. Add 3 tablespoons of the olive oil, the carrot, celery, onion, garlic and a pinch of salt and cook for 15 minutes or until soft, but not brown. Add the anchovy fillets and stir until melted.

Add the chicken mince and give everything a good stir. Cook for 15 minutes or until the liquid has been drawn out of the chicken and evaporated. Add the cloves, bay leaves and thyme and season with pepper.

Pour in the wine and cook for about 5 minutes, until the wine is at a rapid boil and starting to evaporate. Add the chicken stock, then reduce the heat to low and cover with a lid, leaving it slightly ajar. Leave to cook for 1 hour.

Meanwhile, heat a small frying pan over medium heat. Add the remaining 1 tablespoon of olive oil and the breadcrumbs and sauté for 5 minutes or until golden. Remove from the heat and stir through the lemon zest. Set aside to cool.

Bring a large saucepan of water to a lively boil and season as salty as the sea. Add the pasta and cook until al dente.

Add the baby spinach and butter to the ragù and stir through, then remove from the heat.

Drain the pasta, reserving 125 ml (½ cup) of the cooking water just in case. Throw the pasta into the ragù, give everything a good stir and add some of the cooking water if needed to loosen the sauce.

Divide the pasta among serving bowls and serve with grated Parmigiano Reggiano and the lemon breadcrumbs scattered generously over the top.

Chicken stock, Parmigiano Reggiano, butter

There are times in life that call for a dish so simple it can be thrown together without venturing out to the supermarket. This is comfort food at its most basic and one that requires very little of you. It feels silly to call this a recipe, but after a long day, when absolutely nothing has gone right, this is the kind of food you need – aching simplicity.

Feel free to use any stock you like. I tend to use chicken as it is what I always have to hand, but vegetable or beef stock work just as well. As it features so few ingredients, my first choice would be to reach for a fresh stock, but there have been desperate times when all I've had is a stock cube and that's fine, too. This is not the day – or recipe – to be demanding. I've given approximate quantities of stock here, but this will vary depending on whether you are using fresh or dried pasta. If you find you have too much stock, simply discard most of it, leaving just enough to thicken up with the help of the cheese. If you are running low on stock and your pasta is not quite cooked, add a splash more stock or water and continue cooking. You can't really mess this up – and that's what's important here. Cook it to your liking.

The small-shaped pasta used in this recipe means you don't need a fork, as there is no twirling or cutting. It's meant to be to be eaten with a spoon in your trackpants on the couch. And remember that just like your bowl of pasta, bad days end, too.

Serves 1

500 ml (2 cups) chicken stock
small handful of grated
   Parmigiano Reggiano,
   plus extra to serve
2 teaspoons salted butter
sea salt
chilli flakes, for sprinkling
   (optional)
extra-virgin olive oil, for drizzling

FRESH PASTA FOR 1
fregola

DRIED PASTA FOR 1
fregola, risoni, ditalini

Bring the stock to a lively boil. Let's leave it to the stock to be energetic. Season to your liking, remembering that you will be adding Parmigiano Reggiano to the dish later on.

Pour in your pasta and cook until soft and the pasta has absorbed most of the stock – it should be loose with plenty of movement. Notice here I say soft and not al dente like I do in every other recipe. Soft is not overcooked, but cooked enough to not have too much resistance when you bite into it. You want comfort here. Turn off the heat.

Throw in the cheese and butter and give everything a big stir. Your sauce will now look oozy and unctuous.

Season with salt, sprinkle with chilli flakes (if using) and serve with extra cheese and an uplifting drizzle of olive oil.

Bitter greens, chilli, pork crackling

The best part of a pork roast is the crackling, so it's only right that there is a pasta dish to celebrate this. Of course, the Italians have already created such a dish in the form of a stuffed pasta with bitter greens that gets tossed through a topping of chilli and pork crackling. The dish hails from Puglia – the region best known for its deeply rooted 'cucina povera' traditions. This means that the cuisine tends to be simple, cheap and makes use of absolutely everything, including pig skin. In fact, it could be argued that some of the most famous (and delicious) meals were invented by people who were short on time, money and resources, making the most of the ingredients available. This dish is no different: simple, affordable and full of flavour.

You can pick up pig skin from your local butcher or direct from market stall-holders for about $2. Cime di rapa, also known as broccoli rabe, is a bitter green that comes into season in autumn. If you can't find it, which I admit can be difficult if you don't have access to a farmers' market, cavolo nero, chicory, spinach, rainbow chard or kale leaves work just as well. And like the thrifty Italians, if you have some radishes you could also throw in the tops with the greens, which adds a further layer of bitterness and makes use of the whole ingredient.

Serves 4

250–300 g piece of pork skin
2 tablespoons extra-virgin
  olive oil
2 teaspoons sea salt
1 teaspoon chilli flakes
½ teaspoon fennel seeds
2 garlic cloves, chopped
1 bunch of cime di rapa, cavolo
  nero, chicory, spinach,
  rainbow chard or kale, leaves
  stripped and roughly chopped
large handful of grated
  Parmigiano Reggiano,
  plus extra to serve
zest of 1 lemon

FRESH PASTA FOR 4
orecchiette, cavatelli/
malloreddus

DRIED PASTA FOR 4
gnocchetti sardi, rigatoni

Preheat the oven to 220°C fan-forced.

Using a sharp knife, score the pork skin vertically at 5 mm intervals. This helps the heat of the oven and the salt work their way through the skin, drying out the moisture and making your crackling really crisp.

Rub 1 tablespoon of the olive oil, the salt, ½ teaspoon of the chilli flakes and the fennel seeds all over the pork skin and place on a wire rack over a baking tray (this allows the fat to drip down off the skin as opposed to the skin sitting in its own fat). Roast for 45 minutes, then carefully turn the pork skin over and roast for a further 10–15 minutes, until bubbles appear and the crackling is golden and crisp.

If you're like me, resist the urge to nibble the crackling and leave it to cool for at least 5 minutes before cutting up into small shards ready for sprinkling. Now you can enjoy a small piece – the cook's treat – I won't tell.

Bring a large saucepan of water to a lively boil and season as salty as the sea. Add the pasta and cook until al dente.

Meanwhile, heat the remaining 1 tablespoon of olive oil in a frying pan over medium heat. Add the remaining chilli flakes and the garlic and cook for 30 seconds or until the garlic just starts to soften, but not brown. Throw in the greens and toss to coat until wilted.

Add the pasta directly to the greens, along with a 125 ml (½ cup) of the cooking water. Add the Parmigiano Reggiano and lemon zest and give everything a good toss, adding a little extra cooking water if needed to loosen things up.

Divide the pasta among bowls and rain over the pork crackling. Be generous. Sprinkle with extra Parmigiano Reggiano and serve.

Eggs, ham hock

This dish takes its lead from a traditional carbonara, but instead uses a pull-apart, melt-in-your-mouth ham hock rather than guanciale. It's accessible, far cheaper and could be my favourite part of the pig. While I don't want to mess with tradition (carbonara is perfect just the way it is), I do really enjoy the added smokiness of the hock, which is further enhanced by cooking the pasta in the ham hock–flavoured water.

As with all carbonaras, the eggs cook from the heat of the pasta, binding it all together and creating a lovely creamy sauce that coats each strand. Don't stress over scrambling the eggs. The trick is to ensure that the saucepan is off the heat when you add the eggs and to stir quickly. You're not looking for a thick sauce, rather something loose and oozy, so don't be afraid of generously adding your pasta cooking water when stirring in the eggs.

Serves 2

1 x smoked ham hock
(approximately 1 kg)
2 egg yolks
80 g (1 cup) grated Parmigiano
Reggiano, plus extra to serve
sea salt and freshly ground
black pepper

FRESH PASTA FOR 2
fettuccine, tagliatelle

DRIED PASTA FOR 2
linguine, spaghetti, bucatini

Place the ham hock in a large deep saucepan and cover with water. You'll be using this saucepan later to cook your pasta. Bring to the boil over high heat, then reduce the heat to a simmer, cover and cook for 2–3 hours, until the meat is incredibly tender and falling off the bone.

Remove the hock from the pan but keep the water. Top up the water if needed, then bring back to the boil and season with salt ahead of cooking your pasta.

Shred the ham off the bone, discarding the fat and bones.

In a bowl, whisk together the egg yolks and cheese. Set aside.

Cook the pasta in your ham hock water until al dente. Drain, reserving 125 ml (½ cup) of your now ham-flavoured water. Return the drained pasta to the saucepan, but ensure it's off the heat.

Add the shredded ham to the pasta, then pour in the egg mixture and immediately stir until well combined. Add the reserved cooking water to loosen up the sauce and get more movement happening – it should be loose enough to drag a piece of pasta through it. Watch it transform into a silky sauce that coats both the pasta and the ham.

Season with salt and pepper and divide between bowls. Shower with extra Parmigiano Reggiano and serve straight away – there's no time here for Instagram-style shots.

Sausage meatballs, cavolo nero, fennel seeds

If you have never squeezed out sausage meat into little meatballs, then this is going to change your life. It is one of the fastest and easiest ways to achieve flavour and ensures the tastiest and most tender meatballs every time. Emulsifying the cheese in the pasta sauce with a knob of butter is equally life changing, and you'll find it is the secret finishing touch of most pasta chefs.

Serves 4

2 tablespoons extra-virgin olive oil
4 good-quality Italian pork and fennel sausages
1 teaspoon fennel seeds
½ teaspoon chilli flakes
1 tablespoon rosemary leaves, finely chopped
4 garlic cloves, finely chopped
125 ml (½ cup) dry white wine
250 ml (1 cup) chicken stock
sea salt and freshly ground black pepper
1 bunch of cavolo nero, leaves stripped and roughly chopped
1 tablespoon salted butter
handful of grated Parmigiano Reggiano, plus extra to serve

FRESH PASTA FOR 4
cavatelli/malloreddus, paccheri

DRIED PASTA FOR 4
fusilli, penne, rigatoni

Heat a deep heavy-based frying pan over medium–high heat. Once hot, pour in the olive oil. Cut the ends off the sausages and squeeze out small nuggets of meat into the pan. Cook for 5–10 minutes, until the sausage meatballs are golden. Using a slotted spoon, scoop out the meatballs and set aside.

Add the fennel seeds, chilli flakes, rosemary and garlic to the pan and give everything a good stir to ensure the mixture doesn't burn. Inhale its heady scent, an aroma that will linger throughout the meal. Cook for 1 minute, then pour in the white wine to deglaze the pan, watching the bubbles engulf the garlic. Using a wooden spoon, scrape all that sticky goodness off the base of the pan. Once the wine has almost evaporated, return the meatballs to the pan, along with the chicken stock, and cook for 5 minutes for the flavours to meld. Season with salt and pepper.

Bring a large saucepan of water to a lively boil and season as salty as the sea. Add the pasta and cook until al dente.

Now back to your sauce. Add the cavolo nero and place the lid on the pan. Give the cavolo nero a minute or two to wilt.

Drain the pasta, reserving 125 ml (½ cup) of the cooking water. Add the pasta to the sauce, along with the butter and Parmigiano Reggiano. Give the whole thing a firm stir in the pan, adding the reserved cooking water to loosen everything up. Watch it thicken to form a glossy, luxurious sauce that coats the pasta and meatballs.

Serve immediately with extra Parmigiano Reggiano showered over the top.

'Nduja, cherry tomatoes, preserved lemon

I first came across 'nduja high up in the hills of Calabria. We were visiting Rossano, a tiny historic town off the tourist track. As we walked around, I noticed that outside every shop front the owner would proudly sit and beckon you in with, 'I make the best (insert product they were selling)'. When we went up to the butcher, he lured us in with tastings of his famed 'nduja salami. The spreadable spicy salami, made bright red from fiery Calabrian peppers, was the first time I had really tasted heat in Italy – aside from Calabria, most Italians prefer to keep things on the mild side – but it was perfectly balanced by the pork fat and the other flavours. Sure, it was the first time I had tasted 'nduja and I happened to be in its birthplace, but the butcher was right, and to this day I've never eaten better. What I took away from that hillside town was not only a huge piece of 'nduja, which melted into every dish I cooked over the following days, but an appreciation of the pride and confidence Italians have in themselves and their creations. I think we could all do with a little of that Italian pride.

There are very few ingredients in this sauce, which is brought together by the starchy cooking water. The 'nduja is there to add flavour, while the other ingredients balance out the heat. If your 'nduja is particularly hot (always taste it first), balance it out with more mascarpone. Between the salted cooking water, 'nduja and preserved lemon, you shouldn't need to add any more salt. If you don't have preserved lemon, replace it with a squeeze of lemon juice, a little lemon zest and pinch of salt.

Serves 2

70 g 'nduja
250 g cherry tomatoes, halved
2 tablespoons mascarpone
1 preserved lemon quarter,
  skin only, finely sliced
25 g (⅓ cup) grated Parmigiano
  Reggiano, plus extra to serve

FRESH PASTA FOR 2
pici, linguine, tagliatelle

DRIED PASTA FOR 2
bucatini, linguine, rigatoni

Bring a large saucepan of water to a lively boil and season as salty as the sea. Add the pasta and cook until al dente.

Place a large frying pan over medium heat. Squeeze out the 'nduja into the pan and use the back of a wooden spoon to stir and encourage it to gently melt into a fiery red sauce. Stir the tomato through the melted 'nduja and continue to cook for 10 minutes, until the tomato is soft and starting to give up some of its juice.

Drain the pasta, reserving 250 ml (1 cup) of the cooking water. Toss the pasta through the sauce, along with the mascarpone, preserved lemon, about 80 ml (⅓ cup) of the cooking water and the Parmigiano Reggiano. Give everything a forceful stir to encourage the sauce to emulsify, adding extra cooking water if needed.

Divide between bowls and serve with extra Parmigiano Reggiano.

Crisp mortadella, peas, cream

I love frozen peas and will challenge anyone who says a bad word about them. Their very existence makes me happy and, yes, while they are not spring garden peas, their plump bright green little bodies always make it seem warmer than it really is. If it really is springtime, then feel free to use fresh peas after giving them a quick blanch in salted boiling water. Broad beans make a great substitute, but I'd insist on using fresh ones if you do.

Garganelle or rigatoni is my favourite pasta to use in this dish, as the peas and crisp cubes of mortadella fall into the hollows.

Serves 2

2 tablespoons salted butter
120 g thickly sliced mortadella or smoked ham, cut into pea-sized cubes
150 g frozen peas
100 ml pouring cream
½ teaspoon freshly grated nutmeg
sea salt and freshly ground black pepper
handful of grated Parmigiano Reggiano, plus extra to serve

FRESH PASTA FOR 2
garganelle, farfalle, paccheri

DRIED PASTA FOR 2
conchiglie (shells), farfalle, penne, rigatoni

Bring a large saucepan of water to a lively boil and season as salty as the sea. Add the pasta and cook until al dente.

Meanwhile, melt the butter in a large frying pan over medium heat until it foams. Add the mortadella (or ham) and fry for 5 minutes or until just starting to colour. Add the peas and cook for a further minute or until thawed and bright green. Pour in the cream, sprinkle over the nutmeg and season with salt and pepper. Cook for 1 minute or until the cream is bubbling and slightly thickened. Taste and adjust the seasoning if needed.

Drain the pasta, reserving 125 ml (½ cup) of the cooking water.

Toss the drained pasta through the cream sauce, ensuring that the pasta is well coated. Stir through the Parmigiano Reggiano, adding a splash of cooking water if you need to loosen the sauce. Stir vigorously to emulsify the sauce and allow it to coat everything.

Serve with extra Parmigiano Reggiano and another grind of pepper.

Prosciutto, cherry tomatoes, rocket

When my friend Jess and I get together to make pasta, this is the dish we make. We always use fresh tomatoes (preferably cherry), prosciutto (lots of it), wilted rocket for pepperiness and a squeeze of lemon for zestiness. It's one of those dishes that doesn't require much concentration, which is good as we are usually deep in conversation or bouts of laughter by this stage. It can also be made with one hand, which is vital because the other is normally busy holding a glass of wine.

Serves 2

2 tablespoons extra-virgin
  olive oil
1 garlic clove, finely chopped
100 g prosciutto, finely sliced
125 g cherry tomatoes
sea salt
large handful of rocket leaves
1 tablespoon salted butter
zest and juice of 1 lemon
3 tablespoons grated Parmigiano
  Reggiano, plus extra to serve

FRESH PASTA FOR 2
farfalle, tagliatelle

DRIED PASTA FOR 2
farfalle, linguine, spaghetti

Place a large frying pan over medium heat. Add the olive oil and garlic and cook for a minute or so until starting to soften. Add the prosciutto and cook for about 30 seconds, then add the cherry tomatoes and 2 tablespoons of water and season with salt.

Cook, covered, for about 10 minutes, until the tomatoes are just soft and starting to release their juice. Throw in the rocket, butter, lemon zest and juice and toss until the rocket is wilted and the butter has melted.

Meanwhile, bring a large saucepan of water to a lively boil and season as salty as the sea. Add the pasta and cook until al dente.

Using tongs, fling the pasta into the pan, giving everything a good toss. Add some pasta cooking water if needed to loose things up, along with the Parmigiano Reggiano. Toss again, then serve immediately with extra cheese.

Classic meatballs

Making meatballs is a lesson in patience. You'll be tempted to make the balls bigger and bigger as you roll. Bring yourself back to the moment and remember the end game. Oversized meatballs won't be nice to eat, plus they'll require a knife and God forbid you serve your pasta with a knife. So turn on your music. Pour yourself a glass of wine or make a cup of tea. Turn off your phone. This is the time to focus on the task at hand. Be present.

By the way, the meatballs and sauce can be made up to 3 days in advance.

Serves 6–8

120 ml extra-virgin olive oil
1 small onion, finely chopped
sea salt and freshly ground
   black pepper
4 garlic cloves, finely chopped
800 g canned whole peeled
   tomatoes
4 basil sprigs, leaves picked
1 tablespoon salted butter

Classic meatballs
3 slices of stale bread,
   crusts removed
3 tablespoons full-cream milk
300 g pork mince
300 g veal mince
zest of 1 lemon
1 garlic clove, finely chopped
1 small egg
pinch of freshly grated nutmeg
2 tablespoons chopped flat-leaf
   parsley leaves
60 g (¾ cup) grated Parmigiano
   Reggiano, plus extra to serve
1 teaspoon sea salt

FRESH PASTA FOR 6–8
reginette (mafaldine), cavatelli/
malloreddus, tagliatelle

DRIED PASTA FOR 6–8
rigatoni, spaghetti

To make the meatballs, place the bread in a shallow bowl and pour over the milk. You want to leave it to steep for a few minutes. Squish the bread between your fingers to turn it into a wet, milky mush. It feels good and serves as a reminder that your hands are by far the most useful kitchen tool you own.

In a large bowl, mix together the rest of the ingredients – that's the milk-soaked bread, the pork and veal mince, the fragrant lemon zest that's going to lift the meatballs, the punchy garlic, an egg that will help bind the balls, the nutmeg that will add a subtle depth, the parsley for freshness, and, finally, the king of cheese, the Parmigiano Reggiano, along with the salt.

Use your hands again to squish everything together. Listen to the squelch as the mixture moves between your fingers. It's child's play. Remember the joy you used to feel as a kid when you played with playdough? Channel that happiness. Ignite that child within – that part of you who never forgets the importance of laughing for no particular reason, of imagining far beyond what the rational mind can comprehend, and of sitting in wonder at the most mundane. The mixture is now all brought together and ready to be rolled.

Wet your hands (this makes it much easier to roll the meatballs). Use a teaspoon to scoop out a little mince. You want to make meatballs the size of cherry tomatoes. Start rolling, placing each meatball on a baking tray lined with baking paper so they don't roll away. Repeat, checking the size of your meatballs as you go, and don't forget to keep wetting your hands. Savour this slow repetition of action, it's calming. When you've got a tray of meatballs, place them in the fridge for 30 minutes to chill. Just like you.

Everyone and everything is now chilled. Heat a large deep frying pan over medium heat. When it's hot, pour in 3 tablespoons of the olive oil. Carefully place your meatballs in the pan evenly spaced apart. Much like rolling the meatballs, resist the urge to speed up the process by over-crowding the pan. It's only going to catch up with you later. If they won't fit in one go, cook them in two batches. Listen to the sizzle and cook your meatballs until they have a nice brown crust on one side, then roll them over and continue to cook until that crust has developed all over. All up, this will take about 6–8 minutes. Remove the meatballs from the pan and place on a plate. If your pan wasn't big enough to cook all the meatballs at once, repeat with the second batch. This can also be done in a 200°C oven. Now you will probably need to wipe a paper towel over your pan to remove any gnarly burnt bits to get it ready for the sauce.

Pour the remaining 3 tablespoons of olive oil into the pan and add the onion and a generous pinch of salt to coax out the moisture. Stir and cook for 10 minutes or until the onion is translucent and soft. Stay with your pan over this time. I've been burnt too many times by onions. Add the garlic and stir around the pan for a further minute. Now pour in the tomatoes. Fill one of the cans with water and swirl it around to catch all the tomatoey goodness. Tip the tomato juice into the other can to do the same, then pour into the sauce. Tear in some of the basil leaves, reserving a few to garnish the final dish, if you like, and season with salt and pepper. Give everything a big stir, using the spoon to break up the tomatoes.

Leave the sauce to do its thing for 30 minutes, then pop in your beautifully browned meatballs. Take care here, they are still delicate. We want them to hold their shape while they finish cooking in the sauce. Put the lid on, reduce the heat to medium–low and leave to simmer for 15–20 minutes. At the end of all this cooking time, check your seasoning. Add salt and pepper if needed.

Bring a large saucepan of water to a lively boil and season as salty as the sea. Add the pasta and cook until al dente.

Using tongs, pluck the pasta out of the water and drop it directly into the sauce. Finally, add the butter for a glossy shine. Remove the pan from the heat and give everything a good toss. Serve straight from the pan or in a large dish in the middle of the table so everybody can help themselves. Finish with extra Parmigiano Reggiano and the reserved basil leaves, if using.

Slow-cooked pepper beef ragù

Few sights lift the spirit quite like a big pot of slowly cooked ragù. This is the sort of pasta dish you want to crowd around and eat on a cold winter's night. It has a lot of things going for it – its total independence blipping and puttering away slowly in the oven, a salty and rich beefy flavour that you expect from a ragù, and the fact that it pairs perfectly with homemade silky sheets of pasta. If you find that after the cooking time your meat is not easily falling apart, the fault is most likely your oven's – not yours. It just means it needs longer, so cover and throw it back in the oven for another 30 minutes or so.

Serves 6

1.2 kg stewing beef, such as shin, brisket, chuck or blade, cut into 3 cm chunks
10 garlic cloves, finely chopped
125 g (½ cup) tomato paste
2 rosemary sprigs
½ teaspoon sea salt
1 teaspoon freshly ground black pepper
6 anchovy fillets, drained
250 ml (1 cup) red wine
375 ml (1½ cups) beef stock
2 tablespoons balsamic vinegar
grated Parmigiano Reggiano, to serve

FRESH PASTA FOR 6
pappardelle, reginette (mafaldine)

DRIED PASTA FOR 6
if you must, rigatoni

Preheat the oven to full whack (about 250°C fan-forced).

Place the beef in a casserole dish or a deep roasting tin. Add the garlic, tomato paste, rosemary, salt, pepper and anchovy fillets and use your hands to rub the ingredients into the beef. Pour over the red wine, beef stock and balsamic vinegar and cover with baking paper (this reduces evaporation). Pop the lid on or tightly seal with foil. Sealing the dish traps in the steam, which results in incredibly tender meat.

Place the dish or tin in the oven and set the timer for 20 minutes. After 20 minutes, reduce the oven temperature to 160°C fan-forced and cook the beef for 3½–4 hours, or until the meat is falling apart. Skim off the layer of fat that might have formed on the surface, then, using two forks, shred the beef and mix everything together. Discard any chunks of fat.

Bring a large saucepan of water to a lively boil and season as salty as the sea. Add the pasta and cook until al dente.

Scoop out 250 ml (1 cup) of the pasta cooking water, then drain the pasta and transfer to a large serving bowl. Add large scoops of braised beef and give everything a good toss around, adding 125 ml (½ cup) of the cooking water if you need to loosen things up. Stir again and add a little more cooking water if needed. Stir through lots of Parmigiano Reggiano and serve with a little extra sprinkled on top.

Guanciale, tomato, chilli

When people ask me what is my favourite pasta sauce to cook my answer is this one. It's called amatriciana, a simple sauce of tomatoes, guanciale and chilli. Nothing fancy, nothing tricky, just a classic tomato sauce with depth and spiciness. Guanciale is an Italian salt-cured pork jowl, or pig cheek, and you can find it at most delis. If you can't, thickly cut pancetta or speck work well. I use canned tomatoes, and because I make a habit of keeping guanciale or pancetta in the freezer, this pasta can always be a possibility for dinner, which only makes it extra special. The traditional sauce uses pecorino rather than Parmigiano Reggiano, but this book is a far cry from classic Italian recipes so use what you have.

Serves 4

2 tablespoons extra-virgin
    olive oil
1 tablespoon salted butter
120 g guanciale, pancetta
    or speck, chopped into
    2 cm x 5 mm lardons
2 garlic cloves, finely chopped
400 g canned cherry tomatoes
    or whole peeled tomatoes
½ teaspoon chilli flakes
½ teaspoon freshly ground
    black pepper
sea salt
large handful of grated pecorino
    or Parmigiano Reggiano, plus
    extra to serve

FRESH PASTA FOR 4
paccheri, linguine

DRIED PASTA FOR 4
bucatini, rigatoni, spaghetti

Place a deep frying pan or saucepan over medium heat and add the olive oil and butter. When melted, add the guanciale (or pancetta or speck) and cook for 5–8 minutes, until starting to crisp.

Add the garlic and sauté for 30 seconds. Burnt garlic is nobody's friend so keep an eye on it. If you think it's going to burn, quickly dump the tomatoes on top to bring down the temperature and distract the garlic. Once you've added the tomatoes, follow with the chilli flakes and pepper, then season with salt. Reduce the heat to low and simmer for 25–30 minutes, to allow the flavours to mingle and come together.

Bring a large saucepan of water to a lively boil and season as salty as the sea. Add the pasta and cook until al dente.

Drain the pasta, reserving 125 ml (½ cup) of cooking water, and toss the pasta through the sauce. Add the cheese along with ¼ cup of cooking water and toss vigorously to bring it all together, adding more cooking water if needed. Remove from the heat.

Divide the pasta among bowls and serve with, you guessed it, extra cheese and ground pepper.

My bolognese

Every man and his dog has their own bolognese recipe, so I did debate over whether I should include my version. But I came to the conclusion that despite all the variations and differences, the one thing that unites this dish is that it is unanimously loved however it's made, so why not share the way I cook it? The one thing that everyone agrees on is that for the best results don't use too lean a mince, as the fat adds sweetness and flavour. I usually add red wine, but in the warmer months I'll go for white wine for a lighter ragù, but that is, of course, a personal preference so use what you like – or what you have open. I don't add canned tomatoes; instead I enhance the sauce with a concentrated tomato paste. I also add milk to my bolognese to mellow out the acid from both the tomato paste and the wine. I add fennel seeds to my sofrito base, which is probably more Tuscan inspired than Emilia-Romagna, the Italian region where bolognese comes from. Finally, the more cooking time the better – I cook it for no less than 3 hours, but a full day of gentle simmering really gives it an extra something special.

Now to the pasta, which is always a hot issue. Spaghetti bolognese is arguably the national dish of both Australia and the UK, however, you would never see a ragù sauce served with spaghetti in Italy. My feeling on the subject is that it really comes down to personal preference. I do have a soft spot for spaghetti, probably because like most people my age it was a weekly dish growing up, but I do think shorter pastas, such as rigatoni, conchiglie (shells) or fusilli lend themselves particularly well to a bolognese, catching the ragù in all their curves and crevices. For fresh, it's got to be the pasta the people from Bologna intended it to be served with, and that's tagliatelle.

Serves 8

2 tablespoons extra-virgin
 olive oil
2 tablespoons salted butter
1 small onion, finely chopped
2 celery stalks, finely chopped
2 small carrots (or 1 large),
 finely chopped
150 g pancetta, chopped
1 tablespoon fennel seeds
500 g fatty beef mince
500 g pork mince
sea salt and freshly ground
 black pepper
250 ml (1 cup) full-cream milk
½ teaspoon freshly grated nutmeg
250 ml (1 cup) red wine
3 tablespoons tomato paste
250 ml (1 cup) beef or chicken
 stock, plus extra if needed
grated Parmigiano Reggiano,
 to serve

FRESH PASTA FOR 8
tagliatelle

DRIED PASTA FOR 8
conchiglie (shells), fusilli, rigatoni

Place a heavy-based saucepan over medium heat and add the olive oil and butter. Once the butter has melted, add the onion, celery and carrot and cook, stirring occasionally, for 10 minutes. Add the pancetta, along with the fennel seeds, and cook for 5 minutes.

Add the beef and pork mince in batches, allowing it to brown before adding more. Use the back of your wooden spoon to break up the mince and mix everything together. You want to cook the meat for about 10 minutes or until it has lost that raw look. Add a large pinch of salt and a generous grind of pepper.

Add the milk and let it simmer for another 10 minutes or until it has almost bubbled away. Add the nutmeg and stir through, then add the wine and again let it simmer away for 5 minutes before adding the tomato paste and stock. Bring the mixture back to the boil, then reduce the heat to low. You want it to be barely simmering. Cover, leaving the lid slightly ajar, and leave to slowly simmer for at least 3 hours, stirring every so often. If you find it's drying out, add a little stock, but really the end result should be thick and rich. Check the seasoning – you might find that it needs a bit more salt.

When the sauce is ready, bring a large saucepan of water to a lively boil and season as salty as the sea. Add the pasta and cook until al dente. Drain, reserving 125 ml (½ cup) of cooking water. Add the pasta to the bolognese. Toss everything together, adding some pasta cooking water if needed to loosen things up.

Serve with Parmigiano Reggiano scattered over the top.

Bloody Mary lamb, kale

I've been making this dish since I was 21. It featured in my first cookbook and became a favourite with friends. I wrote it when I was going through a big Bloody Mary phase and it dawned on me, one Sunday lunch when I was sipping on one to cure a mighty hangover, that it would work well as a base for a pasta sauce. Pasta alla vodka was a very fashionable dish in the 80s and in recent times it has had a resurgence. Despite vodka having a neutral taste, it does alter the flavour of the sauce with a touch of heat and a sharp bite. Add a splash of Worcestershire sauce and a dribble of Tabasco and you've got yourself a tasty slow-cooked ragù that wants nothing more than to be tossed through some hot, buttery pappardelle.

Serves 6

2 kg lamb shoulder, bone in
2 tablespoons extra-virgin olive oil
1 tablespoon sea salt
1 teaspoon freshly ground black pepper
1 onion, roughly chopped
½ bunch of celery, roughly chopped
2 garlic cloves, finely chopped
800 g canned whole peeled tomatoes
300 ml vodka
125 ml (½ cup) red wine
2 fresh or dried bay leaves
1 tablespoon Tabasco sauce
3 tablespoons Worcestershire sauce
60 g (1½ cups) chopped kale leaves
1 tablespoon salted butter
grated Parmigiano Reggiano, to serve

FRESH PASTA FOR 6
pappardelle

DRIED PASTA FOR 6
conchiglie (shells), rigatoni

Preheat the oven to 150°C fan-forced.

Use a sharp knife to score the fat layer on the lamb at 1 cm intervals, stopping your knife when it reaches the meat. Massage 1 tablespoon of the olive oil into the lamb and sprinkle with the salt and pepper.

Place a large flameproof casserole dish or a deep roasting tin over high heat. Add the remaining 1 tablespoon of olive oil, the onion, celery and garlic and cook for 5 minutes or until softened. Add the lamb, fat-side down, and brown for 5 minutes or until the fat starts to turn golden.

Turn the lamb over to expose the fat and add the tomatoes. Half-fill one of the cans with water and pour this in, too. Add the vodka, red wine, bay leaves, Tabasco and Worcestershire sauce and give everything a good stir. Bring to the boil, then remove from the heat. Cover with the lid (or if you are using a roasting tin, tightly cover with foil) and place in the oven.

Roast the lamb for 4 hours or until the meat is falling off the bone. When cooked, remove the casserole dish or roasting tin from the oven and skim the oil from the top of the sauce. Remove the remaining fat from the lamb and discard. Use two forks to shred the meat off the bone into the sauce to create a thick stew.

Meanwhile, bring a large saucepan of water to a lively boil and season as salty as the sea. Add the pasta and cook until al dente, throwing in the kale for the last 2 minutes of cooking.

Add the drained pasta and kale directly to the lamb stew, then stir through the butter and toss everything together.

Divide the pasta among serving bowls, shower with Parmigiano Reggiano and serve.

Rigatoni mozzarella bake

This is not so much a recipe, but more a set of instructions on what to do with left-over ragù or tomato sauce. The quantities are easy to reduce or increase, so use this as a guide. This dish works especially well with my bolognese on page 193, the basic tomato sauce sans the stracciatella on page 115, the guanciale, tomato and chilli sauce on page 191 and the bloody Mary ragù on page 195, but the list goes on. Really, this works with anything that's going to hold up well when covered in cheese and re-baked. In other words, avoid oil- and seafood-based pasta sauces.

There is a method to my madness in asking you to play with your food and make the rigatoni stand up – it gives the cheese hollow gaps to melt into, which just means an even distribution of cheese. Don't be too precious about this, as long as the majority are sitting upright, you'll be pleased with the result. And who ever said playing with your food was a bad thing?

Serves 2

250 ml (1 cup) left-over
  pasta sauce
125 g grated regular or buffalo
  mozzarella
80 g (1 cup) grated Parmigiano
  Reggiano
extra-virgin olive oil, for drizzling

FRESH PASTA
n/a

DRIED PASTA FOR 2
rigatoni

Preheat the oven to 200°C fan-forced.

Bring a large saucepan of water to a lively boil and season as salty as the sea. Add the pasta and cook until molto al dente (see page 89). You want it to be underdone, as the pasta will continue to cook in the oven.

Drain the pasta and toss it through your chosen sauce – it helps to heat up the sauce here, too. Tip the pasta into a 20 cm x 14 cm or 1.2 litre baking dish and, using your hands, turn the rigatoni so they are standing upright, with the hollow rounds facing upwards.

Scatter over the mozzarella and Parmigiano Reggiano and drizzle with olive oil, then bake in the oven for 20–30 minutes, until golden and irresistible.

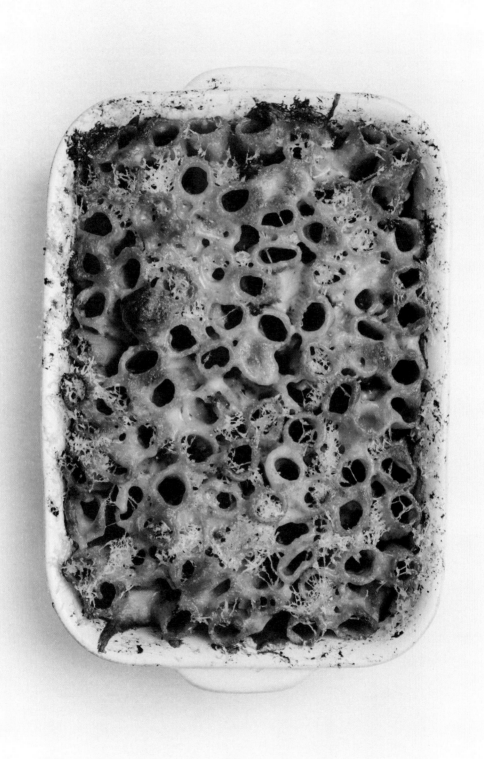

Conversion charts

Measuring cups and spoons may vary slightly from one country to another, but the difference is generally not enough to affect a recipe. All cup and spoon measures are level.

One Australian metric measuring cup holds 250 ml (8 fl oz), one Australian metric tablespoon holds 20 ml (4 teaspoons) and one Australian metric teaspoon holds 5 ml. North America, New Zealand and the UK use a 15 ml (3-teaspoon) tablespoon.

LENGTH

METRIC	IMPERIAL
3 mm	⅛ inch
6 mm	¼ inch
1 cm	½ inch
2.5 cm	1 inch
5 cm	2 inches
18 cm	7 inches
20 cm	8 inches
23 cm	9 inches
25 cm	10 inches
30 cm	12 inches

LIQUID MEASURES

ONE AMERICAN PINT	ONE IMPERIAL PINT
500 ml (16 fl oz)	600 ml (20 fl oz)

CUP	METRIC	IMPERIAL
⅛ cup	30 ml	1 fl oz
¼ cup	60 ml	2 fl oz
⅓ cup	80 ml	2½ fl oz
½ cup	125 ml	4 fl oz
⅔ cup	160 ml	5 fl oz
¾ cup	180 ml	6 fl oz
1 cup	250 ml	8 fl oz
2 cups	500 ml	16 fl oz
2¼ cups	560 ml	20 fl oz
4 cups	1 litre	32 fl oz

DRY MEASURES

The most accurate way to measure dry ingredients is to weigh them. However, if using a cup, add the ingredient loosely to the cup and level with a knife; don't compact the ingredient unless the recipe requests 'firmly packed'.

METRIC	IMPERIAL
15 g	½ oz
30 g	1 oz
60 g	2 oz
125 g	4 oz (¼ lb)
185 g	6 oz
250 g	8 oz (½ lb)
375 g	12 oz (¾ lb)
500 g	16 oz (1 lb)
1 kg	32 oz (2 lb)

OVEN TEMPERATURES

CELSIUS	FAHRENHEIT
100°C	200°F
120°C	250°F
150°C	300°F
160°C	325°F
180°C	350°F
200°C	400°F
220°C	425°F

CELSIUS	GAS MARK
110°C	¼
130°C	½
140°C	1
150°C	2
170°C	3
180°C	4
190°C	5
200°C	6
220°C	7
230°C	8
240°C	9
250°C	10

Writing this book took an army of people and because of that, there are a lot of amazing people to thank. These are the people who have not only made this book possible, but have also been my biggest supporters over the years. You don't often get an opportunity to thank people in print so here goes.

Firstly, to my publisher, Mary Small, for seeing the potential in my self-care ritual. Thank you from the bottom of my heart for your guidance, enthusiasm and faith in Saturday Night Pasta. You made a dream come true. To Clare Marshall, thank you for your patience, advice, sharp eye and general hand-holding. This book is so much better because of the two of you. To Charlotte Ree, no words can thank you for the invaluable introduction to the wonderful team at Plum. You were right; you said they were the best and now I know for certain that they are! Thank you for your cheerleading and belief in Saturday Night Pasta – and for the cookies that fuelled me to keep going. To Lucy Heaver, thank you for making the words on these pages the best they could be and for saving me from grammatical embarrassment. You made it possible to write a book while pregnant and working full time.

To Nikki To, who just so happens to be one of my best friends as well as Australia's best photographer. There are really no words to thank you for everything you did on this book – from capturing the mood and feeling of SNP so beautifully to your support and reassurance, and for always going beyond the call of duty of a photographer.

To the lovely and calming Deb Kaloper, thank you for your beautiful styling and presence. You nailed the effortless pasta plating, these photos would not be half as good without you. Being 32-weeks pregnant at the photoshoot, a huge thanks also needs to go to Claire Dickson-Smith for doing all the shopping and prep for it, as well as cooking with me. A very special thanks needs to go to Jenny Paul from the Old School House in Milton for answering my call for fresh eggs. Jenny drove up from the South Coast to hand deliver the best, most yellowest eggs I've ever seen for the book shoot. The dough is so bright and happy in this book thanks to her lovely flock.

Thank you to Daniel New, who designed this book and pieced it all together so well. I literally fell off my chair when Mary told me that the designer responsible for so many amazing books by people I admire was designing my little book.

To Julia and Pino Ficara from Grano & Farina, my pasta teachers. Thank you for the knowledge, skills, confidence and a wonderful four days in Rome.

To my Fink Family. I am forever grateful for the support, love and opportunity you have given me. I know people harp on about family in the workplace, but there are no truer words when describing Fink – as you can see by the long list of people I want to thank. To Leon Fink, thank you for the ongoing advice and encouragement, and for the curve balls you throw at me. I continue to learn and grow, not only in my career but as a person, because of you. To John Fink, who has been my number-one supporter for more than 10 years, your belief and trust in me and every one of my crazy ideas has allowed me to get where I am today. Thank you for everything you do, say and act for me, I am eternally grateful. To Jeremy Courmadias, your arrival at Fink was a game-changer. Thank you for being the most wonderful mentor, confidante and, most importantly, for giving me my confidence back. To the chefs I feel immensely lucky that I get to work with, and who have shaped me as a cook – Lennox Hastie, who read all my writing after service and always had his comments and feedback in my inbox by morning. For those who don't know, Lennox is as good a writer as he is a chef. Thank you for your encouragement and endless support. To Peter Gilmore, thank you for your support and interest in everything I do. Rolling pasta with you at Bennelong will forever be one of my favourite work memories. To Will Cowper, Richard Ptacnik, Rob Cockerill, Troy Crisante and Tim Mifsud, thank you for always answering my endless cooking questions, supplying hard-to-get ingredients and providing inspiration every day. To our little Comms and Marketing Team – Brigid Grice and Adriana Bradica, you make coming to work each day an absolute joy. We are the sum of our parts and make a bloody good team, if I do say so myself. Thank you for your support and advice each and every day. Brig, thank you for being my sounding board on almost every pasta recipe in here, too – I think I've met my food match. I feel privileged to work alongside some of Australia's hospitality greats and they deserve a mention here: Graham Ackling, Nadine Stegmeier, Trish Rogers, Alan Hunter, Amanda Yallop and Sarah Barker.

To Sophie McComas-Williams and Greta Edmondson, a million thank-yous for your belief and encouragement in both this project and in me. Deepest thanks to Lizzie Meryment, Matty Hirsch and Alecia Wood, whose judgement and friendship I have heavily relied on throughout. To all my friends who have joined in on SNP and been so excited for this book. Your enthusiasm kept me going. A huge thank-you to everyone who got behind the SNP movement and shared their creations on Instagram. Thank you for your kind words; they mean more to me than you will ever know. Special shout out to Instagram friends Anita Manfreda, Katie Graham, Dan Lamond, Sandrine Fourez and Steph Lamb.

To my family. To Mum and Dad, thank you for your limitless love and support, and for instilling a dream-big philosophy. To my twin, Caroline, thank you for your realness and no-bullshit advice – I miss you and can't wait until we can make pasta together. To the Chapmans – Robbie, Pete, Mill and Liv – I think I won the family-in-law jackpot. Thank you always for your words of encouragement and interest in what I do.

Finally, to Tom, who knows my struggle with anxiety better than anyone. I was 15-weeks pregnant when I found out that this idea was going to be turned into a book. Everyone who has experienced pregnancy will be familiar with the rollercoaster of emotions that come with it – pair that with a full-time job and writing a book in a short timeframe and you'll also agree that he deserves a medal. Your kindness, patience and love allowed me to do all three things at the same time. Thank you for navigating that stretch of time with me so supportively. This book is dedicated to you and our little family.

RESOURCES

I am grateful to a number of cooks, books, writers and resources who have taught, shaped and inspired me on my Saturday Night Pasta journey.

- Anna Del Conte, *On Pasta*
- Diana Henry, *How to Eat a Peach*
- grano-farina.com
- Jacob Kenedy and Caz Hildebrand, *The Geometry of Pasta*
- Marcella Hazan, *The Essentials of Classic Italian Cooking*
- MFK Fisher, *The Art of Eating*
- Nigel Slater, *The Kitchen Diaries*
- Nigella Lawson, *How to Eat*
- Oretta Zanini De Vita, *The Encyclopedia of Pasta*
- pastagrannies.com
- Ruby Tandoh, *Eat Up*

205

A Plum book

First published in 2020 by

Pan Macmillan Australia Pty Limited

Level 25, 1 Market Street,

Sydney, NSW 2000, Australia

Level 3, 112 Wellington Parade,

East Melbourne, VIC 3002, Australia

Text copyright © Elizabeth Hewson 2020

Photographs Nikki To copyright © Pan Macmillan 2020

Design Daniel New copyright © Pan Macmillan 2020

The moral right of the author has been asserted.

Design and typesetting by Daniel New

Edited by Lucy Heaver

Index by Helena Holmgren

Photography by Nikki To

Prop and food styling by Deborah Kaloper

Food preparation by Claire Dickson-Smith and Elizabeth Hewson

Colour reproduction by Splitting Image Colour Studio

Printed and bound in China by Imago Printing International Limited

A CIP catalogue record for this book is available from the
National Library of Australia.

10 9 8 7 6 5 4 3 2 1